Bears' Guide to the
Best Education
Degrees by
Distance Learning

Bears' Guide to the Best Education Degrees by Distance Learning

John Bear, Ph.D.
Mariah Bear, M.A.
Tom Head, M.A.
Thomas Nixon, M.A.

TEN SPEED PRESS
Berkeley • Toronto

Other Degree.Net Books:
Bears' Guide to Earning Degrees by Distance Learning
Bears' Guide to the Best Computer Degrees by Distance Learning
Bears' Guide to the Best MBAs by Distance Learning
College Degrees by Mail and Internet

Degree.Net
A division of Ten Speed Press
P.O. Box 7123
Berkeley, California 94707
www.degree.net

Distributed in Australia by Simon & Schuster, in Canada by Ten Speed Press
Canada, in New Zealand by Southern Publishers Group, in South Africa by
Real Books, in Southeast Asia by Berkeley Books, and in the United Kingdom
by Airlift Book Company.

Cover design by Cale Burr
Text design by Linda Davis, Star Type, Berkeley

Disclaimer:
While the authors believe that the information in this book is correct as of the time
of publication, it is possible we may have made errors, which we will correct at the
first available opportunity. We, the publisher, are not responsible for any problems
that may arise in readers' interactions with any schools described in the book.

Library of Congress Cataloging-in-Publication Data

Bears' guide to the best education degrees by distance learning / John
Bear ... [et al.].
    p. cm.
Includes bibliographical references and index.
  ISBN 1-58008-333-1
  1. Education--Study and teaching (Higher)--Directories. 2. Distance
education--Directories. 3. Universities and colleges--Directories. 4.
Degrees, Academic--Directories. I. Bear, John, 1938-
  LB2165 .B43 2001
  374'.4'02573--dc21
                        2001003849

First printing this edition, 2001
Printed in Canada

1 2 3 4 5 6 7 8 9 10 — 05 04 03 02 01

Dedications

From John Bear:

At last the opportunity to issue a public thank you to the two best classroom teachers I ever had: Aram Tolegian at University High School in Los Angeles, and David Berlo at Michigan State University.

From Mariah Bear:

To Joe, the best teacher a gal (or a third grade class) could hope for.

From Tom Head:

To Maybelle Carwile—my grandmother and a teacher.

From Thomas Nixon:

To Elizabeth, who provides love and support beyond all measure, and to David, Maria, and Sarah, who are my greatest teachers.

Acknowledgments

We would like to extend special thanks to Degree.Net editor Justin Wells; this book has certainly been as much his vision as ours. He has kept us on schedule, cooked our half-baked schemes until they're well done, and, on more than one occasion, translated our inscrutable 4 a.m. wonders into English. Some editors should receive cover credit for their contributions to a book, and Justin is definitely one of those editors.

We owe a debt of gratitude to our five profiled teachers, who have let us all have a glimpse into their world and, in so doing, given us clear evidence that this approach can work. To Andrew Finch (page 77), Cindy Knott (page 101), Raeshelle Meyer (page 23), Brent Muirhead (page 99), and Julie Seek (page 74), we say: Thank you, and we wish you the best of luck in your future endeavors.

We would also like to thank our agent, Laurie Harper of Sebastian Literary Agency, who has once again been our helpful guide through the mind-bending world of contract negotiation; Cale Burr, for designing yet another installment in a series of wonderful covers; Linda Davis, for the beautiful design and typesetting; Joann Woy, for dotting our i's and crossing our t's; and our families, for their support and encouragement.

Contents

About the Authors

John Bear is an internationally known expert in the field of distance education, and has been one of its leading advocates for over 25 years. He has taught at Michigan State University, the University of California at Berkeley, and the University of Iowa, and is the author or co-author of some 30 books, including *Bears' Guide to Earning Degrees by Distance Learning* and *College Degrees by Mail and Internet*. He holds a Master of Journalism from the University of California at Berkeley and a Ph.D. in communications from Michigan State University. He has served as Director of the Center for the Gifted Child in San Francisco and as a consultant to a wide range of clients, including General Motors, Xerox, *Encyclopaedia Britannica*, and the Grateful Dead. Since 1979, he has been an expert witness on diploma mills for the FBI. His other published works include cookbooks (including *How to Repair Food*, co-written with Marina Bear and Tanya Zeryck), computer books (including *Computer Wimp* and *Computer Wimp No More*), and consumer guides (including *Send This Jerk the Bedbug Letter*, an expanded version of his doctoral dissertation).

Mariah Bear has served alongside her father as a distance-learning advocate and co-author of *Bears' Guide to Earning Degrees by Distance Learning* for the past ten years, and is herself the author or co-author of nine books (including *Finding Money for College*). She holds an M.A. in journalism from New York University, and her work has appeared in *New York*, *Village Voice*, and a number of other publications. She currently serves as North American Publisher for Lonely Planet, the world's largest travel book company.

Tom Head is internationally recognized as an authority on distance education, and can legitimately claim to be one of the most nontraditionally educated human beings on the planet. He was homeschooled from K-12, completed his B.A. entirely by distance learning through the former Regents College (now Excelsior College), and now holds an externally earned M.A. in humanities from California State University—Dominguez Hills. He is the co-author of *Get Your IT Degree and Get Ahead* (McGraw-Hill), and has worked as a freelance researcher on three Degree.Net titles. He can be found on the Web at *www.tomhead.net*.

Thomas Nixon is an experienced classroom teacher and a university lecturer in both education and linguistics. He is a contributing editor to *ESL Magazine*, where he writes a column on employment and career issues for ESL teachers. He has taught both in the United States and abroad. He has a Master of Arts in Linguistics/Teaching English as a Second Language from California State University—Fresno, and a multiple-subjects teaching credential from National University (Fresno satellite campus). He is the moderator for *CATESOLJB*, the employment listserv operated by CATESOL, the professional association for ESL teachers in California, and is also a moderator for the new DegreeInfo.com bulletin board, which is dedicated to distance-learning issues. Tom teaches and writes in Fresno, California, where he lives with his wife and three children. He can be contacted at *tcnixon@yahoo.com*.

CHAPTER 1

Teachers, Learners, and the Spaces Between Them

Teachers must think for themselves if they are to help others think for themselves.

CARNEGIE CORPORATION OF NEW YORK

We need new teachers and we need better qualified teachers. We need elementary school teachers and high school teachers, teachers endorsed to teach English as a second language and teachers qualified to supervise gifted student programs, directors of religious education and library media teachers, teachers who can teach students how to use computers and teachers who can teach teachers how to teach. We need them, and we need them yesterday.

The U.S. Department of Education projects demand for 200,000 new teachers per year in the coming decade. The number of qualified elementary school teachers would need to increase by 20%; the number of qualified secondary school teachers, by 22%; and the number of special education teachers, by 59%. Thank goodness you are an aspiring or already working teacher, because we need you.

We wrote this book to help people become teachers, and to help working educators advance their careers. As with many professions, the educator's career path is not a freeway but a toll road, where academic degrees and credentials serve as the tickets to ride. You need a bachelor's and a credential to get started, a master's to focus on this, a doctorate to move up into that.

Earning an academic qualification, however, is a serious undertaking: often expensive, always time-consuming. In fact, for most mature, working adults, the traditional route to a college degree—i.e., attending classes and studying full-time on a college campus—is quite simply impossible.

Most education professionals fall squarely in this category. Teaching is a rewarding profession, but—let's face it—spare time and disposable income are not among the rewards. Teachers and teachers-to-be can't quit their jobs to study full-time when there's rent or mortgage to pay. They can't afford to go into debt paying tuition for such a low-salary profession. They don't have time to commute to night school when they've got families to feed, or volleyball to coach, or papers to grade. Yet, the school district won't raise your salary until you find time to earn that master's degree or those extra units.

Distance learning didn't solve these sorts of problems by becoming popular; it became popular by solving these sorts of problems. It's the perfect solution to the challenges faced by aspiring and working teachers in earning the degrees or credentials they need to reach their career goals.

The advantages of distance learning

Distance learning is all about educating yourself on your own terms: where you choose, when you choose, and within your financial means. Here's how:

▶ **You don't go to class; class comes to you.** Distance learning's defining feature is the ability to complete coursework where you are located, not where the school is located. You can earn a degree from many of the schools listed in this book without ever setting foot on a college campus; other programs are delivered primarily by distance learning but require physical attendance for short periods. For a program to qualify for a place in this book, a student must be able to complete at least two-thirds of it from home.

▶ **You can study at your own pace.** For some programs, you can take as many years as you need to earn the degree. Others may want you to stay on a regular semester schedule, but how you pace your work during that semester is completely up to you. What this means, of course, is that you are better able to fit your education around your schedule, rather than fitting your life around your education. However, this is also the aspect of distance education that requires great discipline; no one is holding your hand to keep you on track.

▶ **You can earn college credits by alternative means.** Earning college credit can be as simple as taking a test for what you already know, or describing carefully what you've already done. Though not a distinctive feature of distance learning, openness to nontraditional methods for earning credit is widespread among distance-learning programs, especially at the bachelor's level. By taking advantage of such credit-earning alternatives as equivalency exams, life-experience assessment, and contract learning, you can reduce your coursework load and spend less time and money on your degree.

▶ **You can save money.** Whether it's through lower tuition, lack of commuting, or the flexibility to work full-time while earning your degree, distance learning provides many means for minimizing the financial impact of your educational goals.

How distance learning bridges its distances

Distance learning is the general term used to describe any form of education where the teacher and student are separated by some physical distance (i.e., not in the same room). It's not a recent invention, having been around at least since Plato sat down and transcribed the dialogues of Socrates (who generally opposed writing things down, believing that it weakens the memory) for wider distribution.

The most traditional kind of distance education, and the sort of distance education you've probably heard the most about in the past, takes place by **correspondence**. Students receive assignments by mail (and sometimes with textbooks, though most universities require students to purchase their own), and then send back the necessary papers for grading. Most courses require students to take a proctored final examination through an approved site local to the student, such as a community college.

How to use this book

Some people like to curl up with hundreds or thousands of pages worth of college profiles and start reading them aloud, one by one, from beginning to end; the poetic repetition and symmetry can bring about a peaceful, trancelike state, organizing random patterns of thought into a beautiful and centered whole. The other 99% of you might rather focus on the programs that are relevant to the current stage of your education career, so feel free to try this:

▶ If you'd like to become a teacher and haven't finished your bachelor's yet, turn to chapter 2 (beginning on page 5).

▶ If you'd like to become a teacher, already hold a bachelor's degree, and want to fulfill state licensure requirements, turn to chapter 3 (beginning on page 30).

▶ If you're already a teacher and would like to earn a master's degree, turn to chapter 4 (beginning on page 37).

▶ If you're already a teacher and would like to earn a graduate certificate, but not necessarily a master's degree, go to chapter 5 (skipping ahead to page 80).

▶ If you already hold a master's degree and you would like to earn an educational specialist (Ed.S.) degree, turn to chapter 5 (beginning on page 78)

▶ If you already hold a master's or specialist degree and would like to earn a doctorate in education, turn to chapter 6 (beginning on page 91).

Most schools in the United States now offer these same courses **online**, using that worldwide network of computers known as the Internet to exchange coursework faster and less expensively than by mail. Online communication methods include email, World Wide Web sites, chat rooms, discussion boards, and streaming video. The Internet is coming to dominate the world of distance learning, and is largely responsible for its boom in recent years.

You'll also sometimes hear about **videocourses** (where lectures are delivered by videocassette, and students send assignments via email or correspondence), **audiocourses** (the same, but using audiocassettes rather than videocassettes), **telecourses** (where lectures are delivered on television through special satellite or public broadcasting channels), and **two-way video courses** (where students, using special technology, actually interact with the instructor during a live lecture).

The profession of education: an overview

Teaching is a satisfying and invigorating career, with lots of room for professional growth and plenty of options for specialization. And no matter which qualification you need for the next stage of your career, distance learning provides an alternative for earning it.

Most people start off as classroom teachers, either at the elementary, middle, or high school level. This requires an accredited bachelor's degree and, for public schools, a teaching credential (though more and more private schools are also requiring a credential). The credential is usually earned after the bachelor's as a separate, one-year program, although it sometimes can be earned in combination with a bachelor's or master's. Distance learning is most developed at the bachelor's level, providing countless ways to earn your undergraduate degree quickly and at minimal cost. In contrast, there are not many options for distance-learning credential programs, largely because of the difficulty of incorporating the student teaching component.

The next logical step for a working, credentialed teacher is the master's degree, which allows the teacher to boost her salary and/or move into a more specialized field, such as special education or administration. (Most states require administrators to have at least three years of teaching experience.) For the typical master's candidate—a mature, working teacher with increasing obligations at home—the flexibility of distance learning is especially compelling.

The Educational Specialist (Ed.S.) degree may be a good option for master's graduates who would like to go even further up the pay scale or specialize in a field other than that in which they earned their master's. (For example, a teacher could earn an M.Ed. in administration and an Ed.S. in guidance counseling.) It generally consists of 12–18 months of post-master's coursework. Although the Ed.S. was originally designed as a terminal degree for teachers who don't plan on earning a doctorate, a few doctoral programs give advanced standing to applicants who already hold an Ed.S. degree.

Finally, there's the doctorate in education, the credential of college professors and school superintendents. Researchers, theorists, and writers in the field of education may also find the degree useful, as may teachers (a few states relegate the highest licensure bracket to doctorate-holders). Most of the jobs that require doctorates also require several years' experience working or teaching in public schools. It is possible to earn an Ed.D. or Ph.D. in education with very little on-campus residency.

"Well, I'll be! The committee done approved my dissertation topic after all."

CHAPTER 2

For Aspiring Teachers Who Wish to Complete a Bachelor's Degree

I'm never going to be a movie star. But then, in all probability,
Liz Taylor is never going to teach first and second grade.

MARY J. WILSON, ELEMENTARY SCHOOL TEACHER

If you want to teach, you need an accredited bachelor's degree. It is the most fundamental prerequisite to a career in education, regardless of what state you live in, and regardless of whether you want to teach in public or private school.

How to choose a bachelor's program for a teaching career

In the long run, it doesn't matter what you major in: You can become a teacher no matter what kind of bachelor's you earn, whether it's a Bachelor of Science or a Bachelor of Arts, whether you major in Spanish, music, or geology.

In the short run, however, your major matters. In order to teach at any public school (and an increasing number of private ones), you need a teaching license (or credential), and what you study as an undergraduate can have a big effect on how easy or hard it is to get one.

Though licensing requirements can vary widely from state to state, most involve at least these two things:

1. the completion of a certain amount of coursework in the theory of education and the practice of teaching, and

2. some sort of proof that that you know the subject area you want to teach.

Chosen wisely, what you major in as an undergraduate can satisfy some or all of these requirements. For example, a bachelor's in history is proof enough, in most states, that you know history well enough to teach it. If you major in education, some of your classes will meet credential coursework requirements. For many states, an undergraduate degree in a cross-disciplinary field such as liberal studies shows that you're qualified to teach language, science, and math in an elementary school classroom.

5

Again, as noted above, these majors are not required for getting a credential. But the right major will save you steps—which translate to time and money—after you graduate. That's when your fellow aspiring teacher who got a degree in something irrelevant—drama when she wants to teach history, or economics when he wants to teach preschool—is taking courses you've already taken, and studying for tests you don't have to take.

So if you haven't completed your bachelor's, and you know you want to teach, or are at least seriously considering it, it makes a lot of sense to design your bachelor's curriculum toward that goal. Depending on what program and major you choose, you can go a long way toward earning your teaching license or credential while earning your bachelor's.

Get focused on your teaching goal

In considering what kind of bachelor's program will best serve your long-term teaching aspirations, start with these questions:

▶ **What are the specific licensure requirements for the state you'll most likely teach in?** *This is very important.* As you've probably noticed, we've been doing a lot of "many states this" and "some states that." We're forced to makes these qualified generalizations because every state is different and we don't know which one you live in.

   Don't choose your major based on these generalizations; find out exactly what your state is looking for. Contact information for all 50 teacher licensing offices can be found in Appendix A on page 105. They'll not only tell you what's required, they'll usually identify particular bachelor's programs that meet those requirements.

   Yes, you can later change your mind about where you want to teach. No, you don't have to commit to a place to live before you've earned your bachelor's. A credential can be transferred to another state (see page 35). If you have no idea where you want to teach, pick your home state. It'll keep you focused on something specific.

▶ **What grade level and, if applicable, which subject area do you want to teach?** Not surprisingly, teaching second grade has different credentialing requirements than teaching high school geometry. By choosing your major to meet the requirements of what you want to teach, you can avoid having to take assessment tests or extra coursework down the road. Aspiring elementary school teachers, in pursuit of what is often called a multiple-subjects credential, are best served, depending on their state, by a major in education or liberal studies. If you want to teach a particular subject in middle or high school, you'll need a single-subject credential, and your best bet is to get your bachelor's in that subject. Again, these are generalizations; you need to check the specific criteria for your state.

▶ **How many credits toward your bachelor's do you already have, and how many credits could you earn for life experience?** If you have already accumulated a hodgepodge of college credit, and/or you're old enough to have racked up some credit-worthy life experience, then you'll want to choose a bachelor's program that's open to alternative and nontraditional ways of earning credit, such as transfer courses, equivalency exams, and life-experience assessment (more on these methods below). Lots of the schools listed in this chapter fit the bill, as distance-learning programs tend to be quite liberal in this respect. Our school descriptions provide specifics.

Your four best bachelor's options

Having at least considered the questions above, if not answered them outright, you can better decide which bachelor's is best for you. Your options fall in one of these general categories:

1. **A bachelor's majoring in education or liberal studies.** If you want to teach at the elementary level, a major in education or liberal studies (depending on your state) may satisfy some or all of the coursework requirements for getting a credential and can save you steps down the line (not having to pass a multiple-subjects assessment test, for example). Distance-learning programs in this category start on page 11.

2. **A credential-track bachelor's program specifically designed to meet a particular state's licensure requirements.** If you want to start teaching as soon as you get your bachelor's, this is the most direct route. You graduate with two pieces of paper—a diploma and a state teaching license—and you're ready to be hired for a teaching job. Bear in mind that many states do not offer this option. Distance-learning programs in this category, described later in this chapter starting on page 19, are available in Alabama (Judson College), Arizona (Prescott College), Florida (Nova Southeastern University), Indiana (St. Mary-of-the-Woods College), and Oklahoma (Oral Roberts University). Prospective teachers wanting to get licensed in other states *might* also be able to use one of these programs; in the next chapter, on page 35, we offer some advice on transferring a credential from one state to another.

3. **An individualized or flexible bachelor's program.** A common approach for distance-learning schools, this kind of bachelor's allows you to design your own curriculum and major. The advantage of such nontraditional programs is twofold: 1) you can really tailor your study toward your state's specific licensure requirements, and 2) as part of their flexible nature, such programs tend to be open to alternative ways of earning credit. As noted above, those who have already earned some college credit or have life experience that could count for college credit are best able to take advantage of these programs' flexibility.

Two happy graduates of the highly successful
"Yoga in the Classroom" program.

Common Single-Subject Teaching Areas for Middle and High School Teachers

Agriculture	English	Industrial and	Mathematics
Art	ESL	technology education	Music
Biology	Health science	Languages other than	Physical education
Business	History	English (Spanish,	Physics
Chemistry	Home economics	French, etc.)	Social science

4. **A non-credential, non-education-related bachelor's majoring in an academic subject.** This is the most common option for junior high and high school teachers, who generally earn a bachelor's in the subject they teach and relegate all or most of their education coursework to a post-bachelor's credential program (see the next chapter for a listing of these). Of course, in this book we don't have room to list the hundreds of distance-learning bachelor's programs that can be earned in such fields as English, math, or chemistry, but you can find a comprehensive list of them in our mother book, *Bears' Guide to Earning Degrees by Distance Learning*, also by Ten Speed Press. For more information on this book, see *www.degree.net*.

Earning a Bachelor's Degree by Distance Learning

Earning a bachelor's can be a very intimidating process, but it's not nearly as intimidating as it sometimes seems, thanks largely to distance learning and other forms of nontraditional education. So before we move on to listing the programs, let us bust three myths that tend to thwart prospective students' efforts to earn or complete a college degree.

Myth #1: "Anybody who wants to earn her degree will need to either quit work and spend four years on it, or study part-time and spend six years."

This is true only if you have no prior college credit, no professional certifications, no military training, no on-the-job or volunteer experience, and no significant knowledge of any academic subjects. *Any* of these factors can reduce the amount of time you'll need to spend on your bachelor's degree.

▶ **Prior college credit:** Some schools in this chapter (such as Charter Oak State College, Excelsior College, and Thomas Edison State College) will accept an *unlimited* number of college credits from any regionally accredited university, which means that earning your degree can literally be as easy as having your transcripts compiled in one place; most of the rest will let you at least transfer in the first two years of study (60 semester hours, an associate's degree, or the equivalent).

▶ **Professional certifications and military training:** Most of the U.S.-based schools in this chapter will award at least some credit for professional certifications and military training, either by 1) using the guidelines established by the American Council on Education (ACE), which publishes an annual series of books on recommended credit for professional certifications and military training, or 2) evaluating professional certifications or documented military training as part of a prior learning/portfolio assessment (see below).

▶ **On-the-job or volunteer experience:** Many schools (such as Andrews University, Empire State College, and Thomas Edison State College) award credit by *portfolio* (also called prior learning assessment). The portfolio process simply involves documenting prior learning and matching it up to the requirements of a given for-credit course. For example, a fluent native Spanish speaker would be able to jump through a few hoops and receive credit for at least Spanish 101, 102, 201, and 202. Someone who successfully operated a nonprofit organization for ten years would be able to challenge a variety of management courses on the basis of her professional experience. If you played in a garage band in the '70s, you might be able to challenge classes on beginning, intermediate, and folk guitar.

▶ **Knowledge of academic subjects:** By taking multiple-choice examinations, you can demonstrate equivalent knowledge in almost any popular field of study, from calculus to business mathematics to geography. *At some schools, it is possible to earn an entire degree through multiple-choice examinations.* The three most widely accepted credit-by-examination series are listed below with contact information. Before signing up for any examinations, be sure that your school will accept it for credit and apply it toward your degree. Also, be sure to ask if any other standardized examination series are accepted; many schools offer examinations of their own creation, or participate in a lesser-known standardized examination program.

COLLEGE LEVEL EXAMINATION PROGRAM (CLEP)
P.O. Box 6600
Princeton, NJ 08541-6600
Phone: (609) 771 7865
Fax: (609) 771 7088
Web site: www.collegeboard.com/clep
Email: clep@info.collegeboard.com

The largest standardized credit-by-examination program in the world; almost every U.S. university will accept at least a few CLEP examinations for varying amounts credit. The subject-specific exams, covering dozens of fields (American literature, macroeconomics, trigonometry, etc.), are designed to correspond to typical one-semester or full-year introductory-level courses offered at a university. Examinations, about $50 each, can be proctored at most community colleges and four-year colleges, military bases, and Sylvan Learning Centers worldwide.

DANTES SUBJECT STANDARDIZED TEST (DANTES)
Educational Testing Service
Rosedale Road
Princeton, NJ 08541
Phone: (609) 720 6740
Web site: www.getcollegecredit.com
Email: dsst@chauncey.com

The military's version of the CLEP program, and now available to civilians as well (civilians pay $35 per exam; military personnel may take as many examinations as they like for free). Accepted by thousands of colleges and universities worldwide. DANTES exams tend to be more specific than CLEP exams and are available in diverse fields such as business mathematics, world religions, and human/cultural geography. Proctored at military bases worldwide, as well as many community and four-year colleges, and at Sylvan Learning Centers.

EXCELSIOR COLLEGE EXAMINATIONS (ECE)
Test Administration Office
c/o Excelsior College
7 Columbia Circle
Albany, NY 12203-5159
Phone: (518) 464 8500 • (888) 723 9267
Fax: (518) 464 8777
Web site: www.excelsior.edu
Email: testadmn@excelsior.edu

Formerly known as Regents College Examinations (RCE), and probably still listed as such at some participating universities. Cost is $200 per exam for civilians, but military personnel may take ECE examinations for free. Proctored at community or four-year colleges, military bases, and Sylvan Learning Centers.

Myth #2: "An average on-campus bachelor's can cost tens of thousands of dollars; I can't possibly afford to finish my degree."

This is a very real problem, but there are three very real solutions:

1. **Find an inexpensive program.** Charter Oak State College will let you finish your bachelor's for only a couple thousand dollars; Excelsior College and Thomas Edison State College are very much in the same ballpark. Shop around.

2. **Earn your credit through inexpensive means.** Credit earned through examination, portfolio, or certification/military training assessment (see above) can usually be earned *very* inexpensively. CLEP examinations can be used to wipe out foundation requirements in a hurry, and DANTES examinations can be used to fill in the gaps. At Charter Oak State College, it is quite possible to finish your bachelor's and end up paying something in the neighborhood of $2,500.

3. **Get help.** In Appendix F (the bibliography), we list plenty of books—including John and Mariah Bear's *Finding Money for College*—that detail how to get financial aid through nontraditional means, including employer assistance and student loans.

Myth #3: "If I earn my bachelor's degree nontraditionally, nobody will consider me a real college graduate."

Most people will, though some people probably won't; the only thing that's certain is that if you don't earn a bachelor's degree somehow, this will be a moot point. Besides, nontraditional degrees can be quite marketable; while little empirical data is available on just how marketable nontraditional bachelor's programs are, students who finished nontraditional bachelor's programs through Excelsior College and Thomas Edison State College (see below) have successfully applied to a number of Ivy League graduate programs, law schools, and even medical schools. With Harvard, Stanford, Cambridge, Oxford, and Columbia offering distance-learning classes and/or degree programs, any stigma associated with distance learning, however much of it there is, is certainly in the process of dwindling.

We *do* recommend this: If you end up designing your own program or specialization in a popular field, make sure that your degree plan incorporates the common body of knowledge of a traditional degree program in that field. When in doubt, err on the side of more, rather than less, rigor; if your individualized B.A. in education has the same course distribution requirements as Harvard's bachelor's degree in the field, it should be pretty hard to discredit your degree's worth.

And we can't impress this enough: If you plan on applying your bachelor's degree toward a teaching credential, contact the relevant state department (see Appendix A) and verify *in writing* that the degree will uncontroversially fulfill your state's licensure requirements.

I've been to 47 different schools and these are my transcripts.

We've divided our bachelor's program listings into three groups:

► Bachelor's programs in education or an education-related field (beginning on this page)

► Credential-track bachelor's programs specifically designed to meet a particular state's licensure requirements (starting on page 19)

► Individualized bachelor's programs that can be tailored to education or an education-related field (starting on page 20)

Key to listings

NAME OF SCHOOL
Postal Address (*United States if country not specified*)
Web site URL
Email address
Phone • Tollfree phone (*If a U.S. number, country code (+1) not included*)
Fax
Year founded
Ownership Proprietary or nonprofit (state, independent, or church)
Accreditation Type of accreditation (regional, national, or non-U.S. equivalent) and responsible agency. All schools listed in this book have proper accreditation. See Appendix C for a more thorough explanation of this concept.
Residency Amount of on-campus attendance required
Cost Subjective interpretation of school's relative cost: $ (dirt cheap) to $$$$$ (expensive)
Special fields Fields of study, if other than general education
Description Specific information on the school's offerings

Bachelor's Programs in Education or an Education-Related Field

Readers will no doubt note that the programs in this category are quite international. Will an undergraduate degree from a foreign university present any problems for an aspiring teacher in the American system? As a rule, no. Great care has been taken in choosing every school in this book—U.S. and non-U.S.—and it would be surprising for a degree from any one of them not to be accepted in any context.

Of course, if you're ever unsure about the usefulness of a degree for your teaching career, check with your state teacher licensing office. The licensing offices in New York, California, and Texas told us that a foreign degree would be acceptable in those states provided that the teaching credential was earned within the U.S.

ATLANTIC UNION COLLEGE
South Lancaster, MA 01561
Web site: www.atlanticuc.edu
Email: adp@atlanticuc.edu
Phone: (978) 368 2300 • (800) 282 2030
Fax: (978) 368 2514
Year founded: 1882
Ownership: Nonprofit, church
Accreditation: Regional (New England Association of Schools and Colleges)
Residency: Intensive 9–11 day residencies to begin each semester
Cost: $$$$
Special fields: Early childhood & elementary education, physical education

Special fields in education

Some bachelor's programs in this chapter focus on a particular aspect of education, and can prepare you for a specialized job in the field:

▶ **Adult Education:** If you plan to teach noncredit enrichment courses, or GED prep courses for adult students, you may well find yourself in a situation where public school certification just isn't an issue. In this sort of scenario, a bachelor's in adult education might be a more appropriate—and marketable—resume item.

▶ **Educational Administration:** If you don't plan on teaching at all, and would like to proceed straight to administrative positions, this is probably the perfect degree to get.

▶ **Library Science:** A useful degree for those who would like to work as a school librarian.

▶ **Religious Education:** If you'd like to work as a Director of Religious Education at a large church, or to teach religion classes at a private religious school, a bachelor's in religious education would be very useful.

▶ **Special Education:** A useful degree for those who would like to teach students with special needs: children with learning disabilities, for example.

Offers B.S. programs in education (with emphasis in early childhood and elementary education) and physical education through the Adult Degree Program (ADP). Coursework is organized around a series of eight 6-month "modules," each beginning with a 9–11 day intensive on-campus residency. A student who finishes one module every six months will need four years to complete the program, while a student who takes on two modules concurrently can finish the program in two years.

BROCK UNIVERSITY
500 Glenridge Avenue
St. Catherine's, Ontario L2S 3A1
Canada
Web site: adult.ed.brocku.ca
Email: liaison@dewey.ed.brocku.ca
Phone: +1 (905) 688 5550
Year founded: 1964
Ownership: Nonprofit, state
Accreditation: Non-U.S. equivalent
Residency: None
Cost: $$$
Special fields: Adult education
The nonlicensure B.Ed. in adult education can be completed entirely by distance learning through a mix of online- and videocassette-based study. A substantial

amount of transfer credit may be applied toward the program, and a special accelerated track is available for students who already hold a bachelor's degree in another field.

BRUNEL UNIVERSITY
Department of Education
Uxbridge
Middlesex UB8 3PH
United Kingdom
Web site: www.brunel.ac.uk
Email: admissions@brunel.ac.uk
Phone: +44 (20) 8891 0121
Fax: +44 (20) 8744 2960
Year founded: 1966
Ownership: Nonprofit
Accreditation: Non-U.S. equivalent
Residency: None
Cost: $$$
Special fields: Youth & community studies
The Honours B.A. in youth and community studies is intended for students who already have a strong background in youth and community work. It is comprised of eight modules: information technology, management in youth work, marketing and public relations, research methods and special exercise, sociology and society, and staff development and training.

CENTRAL QUEENSLAND UNIVERSITY

Bruce Highway
Rockhampton, Queensland 4702
Australia
Web site: www.dflc.cqu.edu.au
Email: m.f.kennedy@cqu.edu.au
Phone: +61 (7) 4930 9305
Year founded: 1967
Ownership: Nonprofit
Accreditation: Non-U.S. equivalent
Residency: None
Cost: $$
Special fields: Early childhood education, secondary vocational education, vocational education & training

Offers a B.Ed. in early childhood education, a Bachelor of Vocational Education and Training, and a Bachelor of Vocational Education in secondary vocational education entirely through distance learning. All courses are available via correspondence, and many may now be completed through online study. The B.V.E. in secondary vocational education meets the requirements of the Queensland Board of Teacher Registration; the B.Ed. in early childhood education and the Bachelor of Vocational Education and Training are nonlicensure programs. Each program generally takes about six years to complete through part-time study.

CHARLES STURT UNIVERSITY

International Division
Locked Bag 676
Wagga Wagga, New South Wales 2678
Australia
Web site: www.csu.edu.au
Email: inquiry@csu.edu.au
Phone: +61 (2) 6933 2666
Fax: +61 (2) 6933 2799
Year founded: 1989
Ownership: Nonprofit
Accreditation: Non-U.S. equivalent
Residency: None
Cost: $$
Special fields: Early childhood education, primary education, vocational education

Offers a B.Ed. in vocational education, Bachelor of Primary Education Studies, Bachelor of Teaching (birth to five years), and Bachelor of Vocational Education and Training entirely through online or correspondence study, and post-service B.Ed. degrees in early childhood or primary education. The post-service B.Ed. qualifies teachers for fourth-year certification in New South Wales, though students must already hold basic teaching certification to qualify.

CONCORDIA UNIVERSITY

275 Syndicate Street North
St. Paul, MN 55104
Web site: www.csp.edu/hspd
Email: schoolage@luther.csp.edu
Phone: (651) 641 8897 • (800) 211 3370
Fax: (651) 603 6144
Year founded: 1893
Accreditation: Regional (North Central Association of Colleges and Schools)
Ownership: Nonprofit, church
Residency: One 5-day orientation residency
Cost: $$$$
Special fields: Child & youth development, school-age child care

The School of Human Services offers online B.S. completion programs in child development for early childhood educators, school-age care, and youth development; these programs are designed for students who have already earned at least 56 semester hours of credit from a regionally accredited school. The degrees follow an online cohort model: a group of 10–15 students attend an initial five-day residential workshop, then complete the remaining coursework online, graduating as a group after two years of study.

CURTIN UNIVERSITY OF TECHNOLOGY

G.P.O. Box U 1987
Perth, Western Australia 6845
Australia
Web site: www.curtin.edu.au
Email: customer-service@curtin.edu.au
Fax: +61 (8) 9266 9266
Year founded: 1967
Ownership: Nonprofit
Accreditation: Non-U.S. equivalent
Residency: None
Cost: $$

The B.Ed. "conversion" program is designed for qualified Australian teachers who already hold a three-year B.A. and would like to upgrade their skills (and may be useful for licensed U.S. teachers who seek further study but do not feel prepared for a master's). The program is highly flexible and can be completed entirely by correspondence and online study.

DEAKIN UNIVERSITY

Deakin International
336 Glenferrie Road
Malvern, Victoria 3144
Australia
Web site: www.deakin.edu.au
Phone: +61 (3) 9244 5095

Fax: +61 (3) 9244 5094
Year founded: 1974
Ownership: Nonprofit
Accreditation: Non-U.S. equivalent
Residency: None
Cost: $$
Special fields: Primary & secondary education

The Bachelor of Teaching in primary and secondary education "is designed to prepare graduates with an approved undergraduate degree, for teaching in both primary and secondary schools"; it can be completed entirely by correspondence in about two years of full-time study, or three to four years of part-time study. A B.Ed. "conversion" program is also available for students who already hold a three-year bachelor's and wish to upgrade to a four-year credential.

EASTERN OREGON UNIVERSITY

Division of Distance Education (DDE)
1 University Boulevard
La Grande, OR 97850-2889
Web site: www2.eou.edu/dde
Email: jhart@eou.edu
Phone: (541) 962 3614 • (800) 452 8639
Fax: (541) 962 3627
Year founded: 1929
Ownership: Nonprofit, state
Accreditation: Regional (Northwest Association
    of Schools and Colleges)
Residency: None
Cost: $$$
Special fields: Physical education

The B.S. in health and physical education can be completed entirely through online- or correspondence-based study. In addition to the 30-semester-hour core component, students must complete a 30-hour specialization in athletic training, health, or physical education. A substantial amount of transfer credit may be applied toward lower-level course requirements.

EDITH COWAN UNIVERSITY

International Students Office
Claremont, Western Australia 6010
Australia
Web site: www.cowan.edu.au
Email: extstudi@echidna.cowan.edu.au
Phone: +61 (9) 273 8681
Year founded: 1990
Ownership: Nonprofit
Accreditation: Non-U.S. equivalent
Residency: None
Cost: $$
Special fields: Youth work

The three-year Bachelor of Social Science in youth work can be completed entirely by correspondence; a growing number of courses are also available online.

FLINDERS UNIVERSITY

G.P.O. Box 2100
Adelaide, South Australia 5001
Australia
Web site: www.flinders.edu.au
Email: intl.office@flinders.edu.au
Phone: +61 (8) 201 2727 • (800) 686 3562
Fax: +61 (8) 201 3177
Year founded: 1966
Ownership: Nonprofit
Accreditation: Non-U.S. equivalent
Residency: None
Cost: $$
Special fields: Special education

The B.Ed. in special education can be completed entirely through correspondence and online study over a period of two years full-time, three to five years part-time. The program can be focused on junior primary to primary (U.S. grades K–6) special education, or on late primary and secondary (U.S. grades 6–12) special education.

GLOBAL UNIVERSITY OF THE ASSEMBLIES OF GOD

1211 S. Glenstone Avenue
Springfield, MO 65804
Web site: www.globaluniversity.edu
Email: info@globaluniversity.edu
Phone: (800) 443 1083
Fax: (417) 862 0863
Year founded: 2000
Ownership: Nonprofit, church
Accreditation: Distance Education and
    Training Council (DETC)
Residency: None
Cost: $$
Special fields: Religious education

The B.A. in religious education involves a 36-hour major in religious education, a 26-hour component in Bible study, and a 14-hour component in theology. The entire program can be completed through a mix of online and correspondence study; a substantial amount of transfer credit may be accepted. A special "second B.A." program, requiring only 50 hours of coursework (31 hours in religious education, 12 hours in Bible, and 7 hours in theology/missions) is designed for students who already hold an accredited bachelor's degree in another field.

GRIFFITH UNIVERSITY

Nathan
Queensland 4111
Australia
Web site: www.gu.edu.au
Email: student_enquiry@gu.edu.au
Phone: +61 (7) 3382 1339
Ownership: Nonprofit
Accreditation: Non-U.S. equivalent
Residency: None
Cost: $$
Special fields: Adult & vocational education
Offers a Bachelor of Adult and Vocational Education
(B.Ad.V.E.) that can be completed entirely through a
mix of online and correspondence study. The program
can be focused on adult and vocational teaching, adult
literacy and numeracy, or human resource develop-
ment, and takes four to nine years to complete.

GRIGGS UNIVERSITY

12501 Old Columbia Pike
Silver Spring, MD 20904-6600
Web site: www.griggs.edu
Phone: (301) 680 6570 • (800) 782 4769
Fax: (301) 680 5157
Year founded: 1909
Ownership: Nonprofit, church
Accreditation: Distance Education and Training
  Council (DETC)
Residency: None
Cost: $$
Special fields: Religious education
The B.S. in religious education involves a 52-semester-
hour major comprised of 22 hours of coursework in
psychology and education, 24 hours in Bible study,
and 6 hours in Christian theology.

MACQUARIE UNIVERSITY

Centre for Open Education
Building X5B
Sydney, New South Wales 2109
Australia
Web site: www.coe.mq.edu.au
Email: coe@mq.edu.au
Phone: +61 (2) 9850 7470
Fax: +61 (2) 9850 7480
Year founded: 1964
Ownership: Nonprofit
Accreditation: Non-U.S. equivalent
Residency: None
Cost: $$
Special fields: Early childhood education

The external B.Ed. in early childhood education is
designed for licensed teachers who wish to advance to
the fourth-year B.Ed. level and gain special training in
K–3 education. It is comprised of four modules: the
child and family in society, education and curriculum,
management, and liberal studies (electives). The
program takes three to five years to complete.

MARYVALE INSTITUTE

Maryvale House, Old Oscott Hill
Kingstanding
Birmingham B44 9AG
United Kingdom
Web site: www.maryvale.ac.uk
Phone: +44 (12) 1360 8118
Ownership: Nonprofit, church
Accreditation: Non-U.S. equivalent
Residency: Negotiable
Cost: $$$
Special fields: Roman Catholic religious education
The research-based B.Phil. in Catholic studies (emphasis religious education) is comprised of an individualized, faculty-approved research project that can be
completed in about 3 years. Short residencies may be
required.

NORTHERN TERRITORY UNIVERSITY

Darwin, Northern Territory 0909
Australia
Web site: www.ntu.edu.au
Email: marketing@ntu.edu.au
Phone: +61 (8) 8946 6004
Fax: +61 (8) 8946 6644
Year founded: 1988
Ownership: Nonprofit
Accreditation: Non-U.S. equivalent
Residency: None
Cost: $$
Special fields: Children's services
Offers an Honours B.Ed. and Bachelor of Children's
Services through a mix of online and correspondence.
The Honours B.Ed. is designed for students who
already hold a bachelor's degree of some kind. A
mixed-mode (alternating residency sessions and
distance learning) Bachelor of Vocational and Adult
Education is also available. Each program takes three
to five years to complete.

OPEN UNIVERSITY

Walton Hall
Milton Keynes MK7 6AA
United Kingdom
Web site: www.open.ac.uk
Email: ces-gen@open.ac.uk
Phone: +44 (19) 0827 4066
Fax: +44 (19) 0865 3744
Year founded: 1969
Ownership: Nonprofit
Accreditation: Non-U.S. equivalent
Residency: None
Cost: $$
Special fields: Childhood studies

Offers three-year B.A. and B.S. degrees in education, and an Honours B.A. in childhood studies, entirely through correspondence supplemented with online coursework. The Open University generally will not serve a student at a U.S. address, but it may be possible to enroll by establishing a convenience address overseas.

OPEN UNIVERSITY OF HONG KONG

30 Good Shepherd Street
Ho Man Tin, Kowloon
Hong Kong
Web site: www.ouhk.edu.hk
Email: regwww@ouhk.edu.hk
Phone: +85 (2) 2768 6000
Fax: +85 (2) 2715 0760
Year founded: 1989
Accreditation: Non-U.S. equivalent
Residency: None
Cost: $$
Special fields: Primary education,
            secondary education

For licensed teachers, OUHK offers Honours (four-year) B.Ed. degrees in primary education and secondary education entirely by correspondence; a growing number of courses are now also available online.

STEPHENS COLLEGE

School of Graduate and Continuing Education
Campus Box 2083
Columbia, MO 65215
Web site: www.stephens.edu
Email: sce@wc.stephens.edu
Phone: (573) 876 7125 • (800) 388 7579
Fax: (573) 876 7248
Year founded: 1833
Ownership: Nonprofit, independent

Accreditation: Regional (North Central
            Association of Colleges and Schools)
Residency: 7 days (one 7-day intensive or two
            weekend residencies)
Cost: $$$$

Offers a B.A. in education through correspondence courses, online study, and/or intensive seminars. All students must attend a seven-day liberal studies conference (or two weekend seminars) at some point during the program. Credit is granted for transferred courses, standardized examinations, and life-experience learning.

THOMAS EDISON STATE COLLEGE

101 West State Street
Trenton, NJ 08608-1176
Web site: www.tesc.edu
Email: admissions@tesc.edu
Phone: (609) 292 6565 • (888) 442 8372
Fax: (609) 984 8447
Year founded: 1972
Ownership: Nonprofit, state
Accreditation: Regional (Middle States
            Association of Colleges and Schools)
Residency: None
Cost: $ to $$$
Special fields: Child development services, health
            services education, liberal studies

Offers a B.A. in liberal studies and a B.S. in human services with emphasis in child development services or health services education. Unlimited credit can be earned through courses taken at other regionally accredited institutions, prior learning assessment, standardized exams, exams sponsored by TESC, online courses, military and industrial training, telecourses, licenses and certificates, contract learning, and correspondence.

UNIVERSIDAD ESTATAL A DISTANCIA

Apartado 474-2050 de Montes de Oca
San Jose, Costa Rica
Web site: www.uned.ac.cr
Email: vacademic@arenal.uned.ac.cr
Phone: +50 (6) 234 1909
Year founded: 1977
Ownership: Nonprofit
Accreditation: Non-U.S. equivalent
Residency: None
Cost: $$

Bachelor's in education based on about two years of correspondence study, including written units, audio- and videocassettes, online study, computer-assisted learning, telephone counseling, electronic classes, videoconferencing, and more.

UNIVERSITY OF BIRMINGHAM

Edgbaston
Birmingham B15 2TT
United Kingdom
Web site: www.edu.bham.ac.uk/CPD
Email: d.eaton@bham.ac.uk
Phone: +44 (12) 1414 4856
Year founded: 1900
Ownership: Nonprofit
Accreditation: Non-U.S. equivalent
Residency: None
Cost: $$$
Special fields: Special education

Students with sufficient prior credentials in the field and/or five years of professional experience can earn a research-based B.Phil. in special education with an emphasis in autism, emotional behavior difficulties, learning difficulties, sensory impairment, or speech and language difficulties. The degree can be earned entirely through nonresident study (the degree is based on a single bachelor's dissertation). Students without a strong research background are encouraged to take Birmingham's course on research training, which can be completed by correspondence.

UNIVERSITY OF CENTRAL FLORIDA

Program in Vocational Education and Industry
    Training
Department of Instructional Programs
College of Education
Orlando, FL 32816-1250
Web site: www.ucf.edu
Email: distrib@mail.ucf.edu
Phone: (407) 823 2000
Fax: (407) 823 2815
Year founded: 1963
Ownership: Nonprofit, state
Accreditation: Regional (Southern Association
    of Colleges and Schools)
Residency: None
Cost: $$$
Special fields: Vocational education

Offers a B.S. in vocational education and industry training that can be completed entirely through online- or correspondence-based study. A substantial amount of credit can come from CLEP examinations or transferred credit based on courses taken at other institutions.

UNIVERSITY OF NORTHERN IOWA

1227 West 27th Street
Cedar Falls, IA 50614
Web site: www.uni.edu

Email: contined@uni.edu
Phone: (319) 273 2121 • (800) 772 1746
Year founded: 1847
Ownership: Nonprofit, state
Accreditation: Regional (North Central
    Association of Colleges and Schools)
Residency: Significant for elementary education;
    none for liberal studies
Cost: $$$
Special fields: Elementary education,
    liberal studies

Bachelor's completion programs in elementary education and liberal studies are designed for students who have already earned 62 semester hours of credit. The B.S. in elementary education requires significant on-campus residency; the Bachelor of Liberal Studies can be done entirely at a distance with no residency at all. Credit may be awarded for equivalency exams and prior learning.

UNIVERSITY OF PRETORIA

Pretoria 0002
South Africa
Web site: www.up.ac.za/telematic
Email: telehelp@postino.up.ac.za
Phone: +27 (12) 420 3884
Fax: +27 (12) 362 5168
Year founded: 1930
Ownership: Nonprofit, state
Accreditation: Non-U.S. equivalent
Residency: None for B.A.; short for B.Ed.
Cost: $$

The B.A. in education can be earned entirely online or through traditional paper correspondence, with no required on-campus residency; the B.Ed. may require some on-campus residency in the form of intensive workshops.

UNIVERSITY OF SOUTH AFRICA

P.O. Box 392
Unisa 0003
South Africa
Web site: www.unisa.ac.za
Email: study-info@alpha.unisa.ac.za
Phone: +27 (12) 429 3111
Fax: +27 (12) 429 3221
Year founded: 1873
Ownership: Nonprofit, state
Accreditation: Non-U.S. equivalent
Cost: $
Special fields: Educational management, gifted
    child education, guidance & counseling,
    preprimary education, primary education

Offers a B.Ed. entirely by distance learning in any of the fields listed above; all programs can be completed by correspondence, though an increasing number of courses are also available online. No residency is required. UNISA has recently begun to seek U.S. students more aggressively, most notably through its U.S. agent, the American International Higher Education Corporation (*www.aihec.com*). A correspondent tells us that UNISA may also be seeking additional accreditation through the Distance Education and Training Council (DETC).

UNIVERSITY OF SOUTH AUSTRALIA

G.P.O. Box 2471
Adelaide, South Australia 5001
Australia
Web site: www.unisa.edu.au
Email: international.office@unisa.edu.au
Phone: +61 (8) 8302 0114
Fax: +61 (8) 8302 0233
Year founded: 1991
Ownership: Nonprofit
Accreditation: Non-U.S. equivalent
Residency: None
Cost: $$
Special fields: Adult & vocational education, early childhood education

Offers the following bachelor's programs through online study: the Bachelor of Adult and Vocational Education (meeting the requirements of the Australian Association of Adult and Community Education), Bachelor of Early Childhood Education, the B.Ed. in junior primary and primary education, and the Bachelor of Teaching in Anangu education.

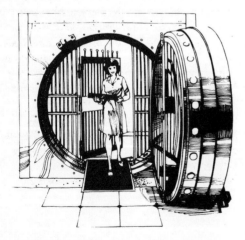

Here at J. Edgar Hoover State University, we take test proctoring seriously.

UNIVERSITY OF SOUTHERN QUEENSLAND

International Office
Toowoomba, Queensland 4350
Australia
Web site: www.usq.edu.au
Email: international@usq.edu.au
Phone: +61 (7) 4631 2362
Fax: +61 (7) 4636 2211
Year founded: 1967
Ownership: Nonprofit
Accreditation: Non-U.S. equivalent
Residency: None
Cost: $$
Special fields: Education studies, further education & training

Offers a B.Ed. (with optional specialization in further education and training) through online study or correspondence, and a Bachelor of Education Studies through correspondence.

UNIVERSITY OF VICTORIA

P.O. Box 1700 STN CSC
Victoria, British Columbia V8W 2Y2
Canada
Web site: www.uvic.ca
Email: srsad13@uvvm.uvic.ca
Phone: +1 (250) 721 7211
Fax: +1 (250) 721 6603
Year founded: 1903
Ownership: Nonprofit
Accreditation: Non-U.S. equivalent
Residency: None
Cost: $$$
Special fields: Child & youth care

B.A. in child and youth care through online and/or correspondence study. Course packages that include printed materials, audiotapes, CD-ROMs, and videocassettes. Instructors lead group discussions using audioconferencing or online chat, and tutors answer queries and discuss assignments by phone and email.

UNIVERSITY OF WYOMING

Child Development/Early Childhood
Child and Family Studies
College of Agriculture
P.O. Box 3354
Laramie, WY 82071-3354
Web site: ecampus.uwyo.edu
Phone: (307) 766 1121 • (800) 448 7801
Fax: (307) 766 3445
Year founded: 1886
Ownership: Nonprofit, state

Accreditation: Regional (North Central
 Association of Colleges and Schools)
Residency: Negotiable
Cost: $$$
Special fields: Professional child development

The B.S. in family and consumer sciences, with emphasis on professional child development, fulfills the guidelines established by the National Association for the Education of Young. All program requirements can be completed online.

Credential-Track Bachelor's Programs Designed to Meet State Licensure Requirements

JUDSON COLLEGE

302 Bibb Street
Marion, AL 36756
Web site: www.judson.edu
Email: adultstudies@future.judson.edu
Phone: (334) 683 5169 • (800) 447 9472
Fax: (334) 683 5147
Year founded: 1838
Ownership: Nonprofit, church
Accreditation: Regional (Southern Association
 of Colleges and Schools)
Residency: None
Cost: $$$
Special fields: Elementary education, interdisciplinary studies, music education, religious education, secondary education

For women over the age of 21, Judson College offers one of the more flexible bachelor's programs in the country. B.A. programs are offered in elementary education, interdisciplinary studies (with an individualized concentration), music education, religious education, and secondary education (with emphasis in language arts or social science). A substantial amount of transfer credit is accepted, and credit may be awarded for standardized or departmental examinations and prior learning. No on-campus residency is required. The B.A. in elementary education is designed to meet Alabama state licensure requirements.

NOVA SOUTHEASTERN UNIVERSITY

3301 College Avenue
Fort Lauderdale, FL 33314
Web site: www.nova.edu
Email: cwis@nova.edu
Phone: (954) 262 8500 • (800) 541 6682

Year founded: 1964
Ownership: Nonprofit, independent
Accreditation: Regional (Southern Association
 of Colleges and Schools)
Residency: Seminars
Cost: $$$
Special fields: Early childhood education, elementary education, exceptional education, middle school science, secondary education

Offers a field-based B.S. in education in the specialization fields listed above, most of them approved, or under review, by the Florida Department of Education as teaching credential programs. Study takes place primarily by distance learning, with frequent weekend residencies at Nova's extension sites (12 in Florida and 1 in Las Vegas, Nevada).

ORAL ROBERTS UNIVERSITY

ORU Adult Learning Service Center
ATTN: SLLE Admissions
7777 S. Lewis Avenue
Tulsa, OK 74171
Web site: www.oru.edu
Email: slle@oru.edu
Phone: (800) 643 7976
Year founded: 1965
Ownership: Nonprofit, independent
Accreditation: Regional (North Central
 Association of Colleges and Schools)
Residency: None
Cost: $$$
Special fields: Elementary Christian
 school education

Offers a B.S. completion program in elementary Christian school education that can be completed entirely by distance learning. The program is designed to meet Oklahoma state licensure requirements, and the school's Web site suggests that the program may meet licensure requirements in other states as well. Credit is awarded for prior learning, transfer courses, and standardized equivalency exams; remaining credit may be earned through ORU's online or correspondence courses or, if the student so chooses, through ORU's semi-residential intensive course offerings. Applicants must be members of the Christian faith and abide by ORU's fairly rigorous honor code (attend church, participate in an aerobics program, avoid tobacco and alcohol, etc).

PRESCOTT COLLEGE

220 Grove Avenue
Prescott, AZ 86301
Web site: www.prescott.edu
Email: admissions@prescott.edu
Phone: (520) 778 2090 • (800) 628 6364
Year founded: 1966
Ownership: Nonprofit, independent
Accreditation: Regional (North Central
    Association of Colleges and Schools)
Residency: Six days (two weekend seminars)
Cost: $$$$
Special fields: Teacher education

Offers a B.A. in teacher education (approved by the Arizona State Department of Education) almost entirely through contract learning and online study; credit is also awarded for courses taken at other regionally accredited universities, for prior learning, and for passing scores on standardized examinations. One weekend seminar is required at the beginning of the program, another at some point during the program.

ST. MARY-OF-THE-WOODS COLLEGE

Saint Mary-of-the-Woods, IN 47876
Web site: www.smwc.edu
Email: adm-smwc@smwc.edu
Phone: (812) 535 5106 • (800) 926 7692
Year founded: 1840
Ownership: Nonprofit, church
Accreditation: Regional (North Central
    Association of Colleges and Schools)
Residency: One day per semester
Cost: $$$
Special fields: Early childhood education, K–3
    education, K–12 education, secondary educa-
    tion, special education

SMWC's Women's External Degree (WED) program allows women the opportunity to complete a nontraditional bachelor's almost entirely by distance learning (with only a one-day seminar required each semester). Credit is available through a variety of traditional and nontraditional means including online courses, correspondence courses, intensive classes, transferred courses, standardized examinations, military training, and assessment of prior learning. The B.S. programs in early childhood education, elementary education (with emphasis in K–6 or 6–12 education), secondary education, and special education are accredited by the National Council for the Accreditation of Teacher Education (NCATE), meet Interstate New Teacher Assessment and Support Consortium (INTASC) standards, are approved by the Indiana Professional

Standards Board, and are designed to meet licensure requirements as established by the Indiana State Department of Education.

Individualized Bachelor's Programs That Can Be Tailored to Education or an Education-Related Field

ANDREWS UNIVERSITY

Nethery Hall
Berrien Springs, MI 49104-0070
Web site: www.andrews.edu
Email: enroll@andrews.edu
Phone: (800) 782 4769
Year founded: 1874
Ownership: Nonprofit, church
Accreditation: Regional (North Central
    Association of Colleges and Schools)
Residency: Seminars
Cost: $$$

In cooperation with DETC-accredited Home Study International, Andrews University offers a B.A. in general studies that can be tailored to education. At least the last 30 semester hours must represent new learning; the rest can be awarded based on transfer credit, prior learning assessment (if the student is age 24 or older), prior military training (based on ACE credit recommendations), and examination (up to 32 semester hours, comprised of CLEP, DANTES, and/or departmental examinations).

ATHABASCA UNIVERSITY

1 University Drive
Athabasca, Alberta T9S 3A3
Canada
Web site: www.athabascau.ca
Email: auinfo2@athabascau.ca
Phone: +1 (780) 675 6100 • (800) 788 9041
Fax: +1 (780) 675 6145
Year founded: 1970
Ownership: Nonprofit, state
Accreditation: Non-U.S. equivalent
Residency: None
Cost: $$$

Offers a three-year individualized Bachelor of General Studies (B.G.S.) that can be tailored to meet Alberta Education Department's academic requirements for a professional teaching certificate.

BRIGHAM YOUNG UNIVERSITY

315 Harman Continuing Education Building
P.O. Box 21515
Provo, UT 84602-1515
Web site: ce.byu.edu/bgs
Email: bgs@byu.edu
Phone: (801) 378 4351 • (888) 298 3137
Year founded: 1875
Ownership: Nonprofit, church
Accreditation: Regional (Northwest Association of
Schools and Colleges)
Residency: Five 2-week seminars plus a 1-week
graduation seminar
Cost: $$$$

The Bachelor of General Studies (B.G.S.) is available
with optional concentrations in a variety of fields
(including family studies, management, psychology,
and writing); although no concentrations are available
in the field of education, it is quite possible to design an
"off-the-record double concentration" by completing a
substantial amount of education coursework and applying it toward the degree as elective credit. Nontraditional credit is granted on a case-by-case basis. Most of
the program can be completed by correspondence or
through online study, but at least 30 semester hours
must be earned residentially at BYU; intensive courses
are offered during the spring and summer. Students
who have already taken on-campus courses at BYU
may apply them toward the 30-credit residency requirement. Although BYU welcomes students of any faith,
all students in the program must abide by BYU's non-
sectarian Code of Honor and receive an annual ecclesi-
astical endorsement.

BURLINGTON COLLEGE

95 North Avenue
Burlington, VT 05401
Web site: www.burlcol.edu/distance.htm
Email: admissions@burlcol.edu
Phone: (802) 862 9616 • (800) 862 9616
Fax: (802) 660 4331
Year founded: 1972
Ownership: Nonprofit, independent
Accreditation: Regional (New England Association
of Schools and Colleges)
Residency: Negotiable
Cost: $$$$

The Independent Degree Program (IDP) individualized
B.A. can be tailored to virtually any education-related
field. Students attend a four-day residential workshop
in Burlington at the beginning of each semester; all
coursework is based on individualized student-faculty

contracts and can incorporate industry or volunteer
projects. Burlington accepts a substantial amount of
transfer credit, and it's quite possible for a full-time student who has already earned 90+ hours of credit to
complete the program in only two semesters.

CALIFORNIA STATE UNIVERSITY—FRESNO

AIC - Distance Learning
5241 N. Maple Avenue
McKee Fisk Building, Room 110
Fresno, CA 93740-8027
Web site: www.csufresno.edu/aic/distance.html
Phone: (559) 278 2058
Fax: (559) 278 7026
Year founded: 1911
Ownership: Nonprofit, state
Accreditation: Regional (WASC)
Residency: None
Cost: $$

The B.A. in liberal studies can be tailored to the field of
education, incorporating coursework from the CLAD
credential and certificate programs (see chapter 3) or
from Cal Fresno's M.A. in education (see chapter 4).
The degree can be completed entirely through a mix of
online coursework and transfer credit.

CAPITAL UNIVERSITY

Columbus Center
2199 E. Main Street
Columbus, OH 43209-2394
Web site: www.capital.edu
Email: rashbroo@capital.edu
Phone: (614) 236 6996
Fax: (614) 236 6171
Year founded: 1830
Ownership: Nonprofit, church
Accreditation: Regional (North Central
Association of Colleges and Schools)
Residency: Negotiable
Cost: $$$$

The individualized B.A. was originally designed by the
Union of Experimenting Colleges and Universities
(now known as the Union Institute) in 1976, and was
taken over by Capital University in 1979. The program
can be completed entirely through a mix of contract
learning, prior learning evaluation, and transfer credit,
and can be tailored to virtually any field (or interdisci-
plinary combination of fields).

CHARTER OAK STATE COLLEGE

55 Paul J. Manafort Drive
New Britain, CT 06053-2142
Web site: www.cosc.edu
Email: info@cosc.edu
Phone: (860) 832 3855
Fax: (860) 832 3999
Year founded: 1973
Ownership: Nonprofit, state
Accreditation: Regional (New England
      Association of Schools and Colleges)
Residency: None
Cost: $

Offers individualized B.A. and B.S. degrees in any field of the student's choice, including education. An unlimited amount of credit is awarded for courses taken at other regionally accredited universities, standardized examinations (CLEP, DANTES, and GRE), certifications, military training, vocational training, and prior learning assessment. Tuition is among the most reasonable you will find.

CITY UNIVERSITY

335 116th Avenue, SE
Bellevue, WA 98004
Web site: www.cityu.edu
Email: info@cityu.edu
Phone: (425) 637 1010 • (800) 426 5596
Fax: (425) 277 2437
Year founded: 1973
Ownership: Nonprofit, independent
Accreditation: Regional (Northwest
      Association of Schools and Colleges)
Residency: None
Cost: $$$

The B.S. in general studies is an individualized program. Students focus on two fields and address them in a cohesive, interdisciplinary fashion. A substantial amount of transfer credit is accepted into the program; a limited amount of credit may also be granted based on standardized examination, military training, or prior learning assessment. All coursework can be completed online.

COLLEGE OF WEST VIRGINIA

609 South Kanawha Street
Beckley, WV 25802-2830
Web site: www.cwv.edu/saell
Email: saell@cwv.edu
Phone: (304) 253 7351 • (800) 766 6067
Fax: (304) 253 3485
Year founded: 1933
Ownership: Nonprofit, independent

Accreditation: Regional (North Central
      Association of Colleges and Schools)
Residency: None
Cost: $$$

Offers B.A. and B.S. programs in interdisciplinary studies comprised of a liberal arts component (63 semester hours) and a career component (66 semester hours). The career component can be focused on health promotion and education, or (with faculty approval) on another field of the student's choice. An almost unlimited amount of transfer credit may be applied toward the program, and a substantial amount of credit may be granted based on standardized examinations and prior learning assessment.

COLUMBIA UNION COLLEGE

7600 Flower Avenue
Wilkinson Hall, Room 336A
Takoma Park, MD 20912-7796
Web site: www.cuc.edu
Email: hsi@cuc.edu
Phone: (301) 891 4124 • (800) 835 4212
Year founded: 1904
Ownership: Nonprofit, church
Accreditation: Regional (Middle States
      Association of Colleges and Schools)
Residency: None
Cost: $$$

The B.A. and B.S. programs in general studies are highly flexible and can be tailored to virtually any field of the student's choice, including education. At least 30 credits must be earned through CUC via correspondence, online study, or contract learning; the rest can be earned via transfer credit, examination, and assessment of prior learning.

EASTERN ILLINOIS UNIVERSITY

School of Adult and Continuing Education
600 Lincoln Avenue
Charleston, IL 61920
Web site: www.eiu.edu/~adulted
Email: lkwoodward@eiu.edu
Phone: (217) 581 5618
Year founded: 1895
Ownership: Nonprofit, state
Accreditation: Regional (North Central
      Association of Colleges and Schools)
Residency: None
Cost: $$

The Board of Trustees Bachelor of Arts is an individualized program that can be tailored to virtually any field, including education. A substantial amount of the program may be completed based on transfer credit, exam-

Student profile: Raeshelle Meyer

Raeshelle Meyer long knew that she wanted to be a public school teacher. However, as so often happens, life intervened. After becoming established in eastern Oregon and getting married, she came to the realization that she needed and wanted to return to school to earn her teaching degree. She now teaches a combined seventh and eighth grade class in Willowcreek, a very rural community in eastern Oregon. She is a graduate of the first cohort pre-service teacher education program provided by Eastern Oregon University through distance education. Raeshelle recently addressed the Oregon Ways & Means Committee regarding continued funding for collaborative distance education programs in eastern Oregon.

Best Education Degrees: Why did you choose the institution that you did?
Raeshelle Meyer: Living in eastern Oregon affords me with a quality of life that I didn't want to trade in order to pursue my dreams of becoming a teacher. Eastern Oregon University's teacher preparation program provided me with options to access a high quality education program without having to leave the region, uproot my family, or attend a school out of state.

BED: Describe your learning experience.
RM: In addition to attending live classes, during the process of earning my bachelor's degree it became necessary to take classes by other means in order to get the credits needed for my degree. I achieved this by taking Web classes, individualized study classes, and weekend satellite classes.

BED: Would you recommend this particular program to others? Why?
RM: Yes, I would and do recommend the CUESTE program to others simply because of the commitment of the professors and staff to provide a quality education and experience. Their interest in me succeeding was shown by their professionalism, dedication, and involvement in my achieving my dream. Eastern's program has made a difference in my life and the lives of others, and has produced exemplary teachers who are now filling a void in rural Oregon.

BED: Would you recommend distance learning in general to others? Why?
RM: I would recommend distance learning to others because of the flexibility that it provides. As the demands on professionals rise, it is of the utmost importance that people have every opportunity to continue their education. In addition, distance learning provides nontraditional students like myself an opportunity to earn a degree and fulfill our dreams without having to make concessions to our families and careers.

BED: What was your primary motivation in earning this degree?
RM: My main motivation for earning this degree was to pursue my educational goals of becoming a teacher. I was tired of earning minimum wage at dead-end jobs and wanted to return to school. I was frustrated that I hadn't pursued my dreams of becoming a teacher. Moreover, I knew that I didn't want to leave my family and needed access to a quality education that would prepare me to become an Oregon teacher.

ination, and prior learning assessment. A minimum of 15 semester hours of coursework must be completed through EIU itself through traditional, online, or correspondence-based coursework.

EMPIRE STATE COLLEGE

Center for Distance Learning
3 Union Avenue
Saratoga Springs, NY 12866-4391
Web site: www.esc.edu
Email: cdl@esc.edu
Phone: (518) 587 2100 • (800) 847 3000
Fax: (518) 587 2660
Year founded: 1971
Ownership: Nonprofit, state
Accreditation: Regional (Middle States Association of Colleges and Schools)
Residency: None
Cost: $ to $$

Empire State College allows students to pursue an individualized bachelor's inexpensively and entirely off campus. ESC accepts an almost unlimited amount of transfer coursework and grants credit for prior learning, standardized examinations, and military or vocational training.

EXCELSIOR COLLEGE

7 Columbia Circle
Albany, NY 12203-5159
Web site: www.excelsior.edu
Phone: (518) 464 8500 • (888) 647 2388
Fax: (518) 464 8777
Year founded: 1971
Ownership: Nonprofit, independent
Accreditation: Regional (Middle States Association of Colleges and Schools)
Residency: None
Cost: $ to $$$

Formerly known as Regents College of the University of the State of New York and a longtime leader in nontraditional education, Excelsior College allows students to pursue a flexible B.A. or B.S. in liberal arts that can be tailored to the needs and interests of aspiring teachers. An unlimited amount of transfer credit is accepted, and credit is also granted based on standardized examinations, military training, vocational training, and nonacademic certification.

FORT HAYS STATE UNIVERSITY

600 Park Street
Hays, KS 67601
Web site: www.fhsu.edu/coas/bgs.html
Email: jmbriggs@fhsu.edu

Phone: (785) 628 4234 • (888) 351 3587
Fax: (785) 628 4037
Year founded: 1902
Ownership: Nonprofit, state
Accreditation: Regional (North Central Association of Colleges and Schools)
Residency: None
Cost: $$

The Fort Hays Bachelor of General Studies (B.G.S.) is available with a student-defined 21-semester-hour concentration and 58 hours of elective credit, allowing the student to effectively tailor 79 hours of the program to a field of her choice. At least 30 hours of credit must be completed through FHSU (through on-campus, online, or correspondence coursework); remaining requirements may be fulfilled through transfer credit, standardized examinations, and prior learning assessment.

FRAMINGHAM STATE COLLEGE

100 State Street
P.O. Box 9101
Framingham, MA 01701
Web site: www.framingham.edu
Phone: (508) 620 1220
Fax: (508) 626 4592
Year founded: 1839
Ownership: Nonprofit, state
Accreditation: Regional (New England Association of Schools and Colleges)
Residency: Negotiable
Cost: $$

Offers a B.A. in liberal studies that can be tailored to education (or virtually any other field of the student's choice). A substantial amount of credit may be granted for courses taken at other universities, equivalency examinations, and prior learning assessment. Some on-campus residency is generally required, and usually fulfilled through a mix of summer intensive seminars and weekend courses or through another arrangement satisfactory to the student advisory committee.

GODDARD COLLEGE

123 Pitkin Road
Plainfield, VT 05667
Web site: www.goddard.edu
Email: admissions@goddard.edu
Phone: (802) 454 8311
Year founded: 1938
Ownership: Nonprofit, independent
Accreditation: Regional (New England Association of Schools and Colleges)
Residency: Negotiable
Cost: $$$$

Offers an individualized B.A. that can be tailored to virtually any field, including education (or a specific interdisciplinary or subdisciplinary field). Up to 90 hours of credit can come from a variety of alternative sources including transfer credit, examination, and assessment of prior learning; at least 30 hours must be completed through Goddard via contract learning or independent study (online or correspondence-based). A negotiable amount of residency is required in the form of seminars.

GOVERNORS STATE UNIVERSITY

BOG Program
University Park, IL 60466
Web site: www.govst.edu/bog
Email: gsubog@govst.edu
Phone: (708) 534 4092 • (800) 478 8478
Fax: (708) 534 1645
Year founded: 1969
Ownership: Nonprofit, state
Accreditation: Regional (North Central Association of Colleges and Schools)
Residency: None
Cost: $ to $$$

The Board of Governors B.A. can be tailored to any field of the student's choice. An unlimited amount of credit is granted for transferred coursework, military training, vocational training and certification, prior learning assessment, and standardized examinations. Remaining credit requirements may be fulfilled through online, correspondence, or television-based courses taken directly from Governors State.

HAMPTON UNIVERSITY

Hampton, VA 23668
Web site: www.hamptonu.edu
Phone: (757) 727 5000 • (800) 624 3328
Fax: (757) 727 5085
Year founded: 1868
Ownership: Nonprofit, independent
Accreditation: Regional (Southern Association of Colleges and Schools)
Residency: None
Cost: $$ to $$$

The B.A. in general studies is a highly flexible program that can be largely focused on education if the student so chooses. The entire program can be completed by distance learning through a mix of online and correspondence coursework. Credit by examination is also granted on a case-by-case basis, and a substantial amount of transfer credit is accepted.

INDIANA UNIVERSITY

School of Continuing Studies
Owen Hall 001
Bloomington, IN 47405
Web site: scs.indiana.edu
Email: scs@indiana.edu
Phone: (812) 855 8995 • (800) 334 1011
Fax: (812) 855 8997
Year founded: 1912
Ownership: Nonprofit, state
Accreditation: Regional (North Central Association of Colleges and Schools)
Residency: None
Cost: $$ to $$$

Students working toward the Bachelor of General Studies (B.G.S.) can design an individualized specialization from the more than 260 courses offered online or by correspondence through Indiana's School of Continuing Studies. A substantial amount of transfer credit may also be applied to the degree.

MURRAY STATE UNIVERSITY

P.O. Box 9
Murray, KY 42071
Web site: www.mursuky.edu
Email: marla.poyner@murraystate.edu
Phone: (270) 762 5322 • (800) 669 7654
Year founded: 1922
Ownership: Nonprofit, state
Accreditation: Regional (Southern Association of Colleges and Schools)
Residency: Yearly one-day seminars
Cost: $$$

Offers a Bachelor of Independent Studies (B.I.S.) that can be completed almost entirely by distance learning and tailored to a field of the student's choice. At least 32 semester hours must be earned through Murray State via online courses, correspondence courses, and/or departmental exams. Other credit may be awarded based on transfer credit, standardized examinations, and prior learning assessment.

NEW SCHOOL UNIVERSITY

68 Fifth Avenue
New York, NY 10011
Web site: www.dialnsa.edu
Email: admissions@dialnsa.edu
Phone: (212) 229 5880
Fax: (212) 989 2928
Year founded: 1919
Ownership: Nonprofit, independent
Accreditation: Regional (Middle States Association of Colleges and Schools)

Residency: None
Cost: $$$

Offers an online B.A. completion program in liberal studies for students who have already earned 60 semester hours (90 quarter hours) or more of credit. No residency is required.

NEW YORK INSTITUTE OF TECHNOLOGY

221 Carleton Avenue
Central Islip, NY 11722
Web site: www.nyit.edu
Phone: (631) 348 3200 • (800) 345 6948
Fax: (631) 348 0912
Year founded: 1955
Ownership: Nonprofit, independent
Accreditation: Regional (Middle States Association of Colleges and Schools)
Residency: None
Cost: $$$

NYIT offers B.A., B.S., and B.P.S. (Bachelor of Professional Studies) degrees in interdisciplinary studies entirely by distance learning. A substantial amount of credit can be earned through transferred courses, standardized examinations, and prior learning assessment. Students may fulfill remaining requirements by selecting from among NYIT's own distance-learning courses, offered online and by correspondence.

OKLAHOMA CITY UNIVERSITY

2501 N. Blackwelder
Oklahoma City, OK 73106-1493
Web site: www.okcu.edu/plus
Email: plus@okcu.edu
Phone: (405) 521 5265
Year founded: 1901
Ownership: Nonprofit, church
Accreditation: Regional (North Central Association of Colleges and Schools)
Residency: Negotiable
Cost: $$$

The Prior Learning and University Studies (PLUS) adult degree completion program allows students to pursue an individualized B.A. or B.S. in a nontraditional manner and, with faculty approval, to pursue it entirely by distance learning. A substantial amount of transfer credit is accepted into the program; credit is also granted based on standardized examinations and prior learning assessment.

SALVE REGINA UNIVERSITY

100 Ochre Point Avenue
Newport, RI 02840-4192
Web site: www.salve.edu
Email: sruadmis@salve.edu
Phone: (401) 847 6650 • (800) 637 0002
Fax: (401) 341 2938
Year founded: 1934
Ownership: Nonprofit, church
Accreditation: Regional (New England Association of Schools and Colleges)
Residency: One 5-day seminar
Cost: $$$

B.A. completion program in liberal studies for students who have already earned 45 semester hours of college credit. Remaining requirements can be fulfilled through online and correspondence courses, prior learning assessment, and examination. All students must attend a June intensive seminar at some point during the program.

SKIDMORE COLLEGE

University Without Walls
815 North Broadway
Saratoga Springs, NY 12866
Web site: www.skidmore.edu
Email: uww@skidmore.edu
Phone: (518) 580 5450
Fax: (518) 580 5449
Year founded: 1911
Ownership: Nonprofit, independent
Accreditation: Regional (Middle States Association of Colleges and Schools)
Residency: Three days total
Cost: $$$$

Individualized B.A. or B.S. with only three days on campus: one for an admissions interview, one for advising and planning sessions, and another for approval of the degree plan. Each program is designed from the ground up to meet the needs of the individual student, and culminates in a final project that demonstrates exceptional learning in the student's chosen field(s).

SOUTHWESTERN ADVENTIST UNIVERSITY

Keene, TX 76059
Web site: www.swau.edu
Email: admissions@swau.edu
Phone: (817) 556 4705 • (800) 433 2240
Fax: (817) 556 4742
Year founded: 1893
Ownership: Nonprofit, church
Accreditation: Regional (Southern Association of Colleges and Schools)
Residency: One 6-day admissions seminar
Cost: $$$$

Offers individualized B.A. and B.S. degrees through the Adult Degree Program (ADP), with only six days required on campus. Credit is awarded on the basis of transfer credit, proficiency exams, and prior learning assessment; remaining requirements can be completed through correspondence and online study.

SOUTHWESTERN ASSEMBLIES OF GOD UNIVERSITY

1200 Sycamore
Waxahachie, TX 75165
Web site: www.sagu.edu/sde
Email: info@sagu.edu
Phone: (972) 937 4010 • (888) 937 7248
Fax: (972) 923 0488
Year founded: 1927
Ownership: Nonprofit, church
Accreditation: Regional (Southern Association of Colleges and Schools)
Residency: Two days at the beginning of each semester
Cost: $$$$

Individualized B.A. and B.S. degrees with two days of on-campus residency required at the beginning of each semester. A substantial amount of transfer credit is accepted, and some requirements may be fulfilled through other alternative means on a case-by-case basis. Remaining requirements may be fulfilled through online and correspondence study. Students must make a statement of Christian faith.

STRAYER UNIVERSITY

1025 15th Street, NW
Washington, DC 20005
Web site: www.strayer.edu
Email: jct@strayer.edu
Phone: (703) 339 1850 • (800) 422 8055
Fax: (703) 339 1852
Year founded: 1892
Ownership: Nonprofit, independent
Accreditation: Regional (Middle States Association of Colleges and Schools)
Residency: None
Cost: $$$

Offers a B.A. in general studies through online study, correspondence courses, and prior learning (transfer courses, credit by examination, military training, and life-experience assessment).

SYRACUSE UNIVERSITY

Independent Study Degree Programs
700 University Avenue
Syracuse, NY 13244-2530
Web site: www.yesu.syr.edu
Email: suisdp@uc.syr.edu

Here, Jawaharlal demonstrates graphically that nothing weighs more than a good home study education (here inexplicably symbolized by three vege-sausages of varying sizes).

Phone: (315) 443 3480 • (800) 442 0501
Fax: (315) 443 4174
Year founded: 1870
Ownership: Nonprofit, independent
Accreditation: Regional (Middle States Association of Colleges and Schools)
Residency: Negotiable yearly residencies of one to four weeks
Cost: $$$$

The B.A. in liberal studies addresses four main study areas: humanities, mathematics, sciences, and social sciences. It is possible to tailor the program to an education field by taking advantage of the special studies, elective credit, and thesis options. A substantial amount of transfer credit may be accepted into the program.

TEXAS TECH UNIVERSITY

Outreach and Extended Studies
6901 Quaker Avenue
Lubbock, TX 79413
Web site: www.dce.ttu.edu
Email: distlearn@ttu.edu
Phone: (806) 742 7200 • (800) 692 6877
Fax: (806) 742 7222
Year founded: 1923
Ownership: Nonprofit, state
Accreditation: Regional (Southern Association of Colleges and Schools)
Residency: None
Cost: $$

Bachelor of General Studies (B.G.S.) through correspondence, online study, or contract learning based on three areas of study, which can all be education-related. Credit awarded for prior learning including transfer credit, life-experience assessment, and credit by examination.

UNION INSTITUTE

440 East McMillan Street
Cincinnati, OH 45206-1925
Web site: www.tui.edu
Email: admission@tui.edu
Phone: (513) 861 6400 • (800) 486 3116
Fax: (513) 861 0779
Year founded: 1964
Ownership: Nonprofit, independent
Accreditation: Regional (North Central Association of Colleges and Schools)
Residency: Negotiable
Cost: $$$$$
Note: A correspondent tells us that the Union Institute will soon be changing its name, but details were not available at press time.

Offers an individualized B.A. program with brief residencies required at one of the Union Institute's learning centers (in Cincinnati, OH; Miami, FL; and Los Angeles, Sacramento, and San Diego, CA). All but 30 of the required hours can be awarded for prior learning (courses taken elsewhere, credit by examination, and life-experience assessment); the remainder can be earned on the basis of online, correspondence, and contract-based study.

UNIVERSITY OF ALABAMA

Tuscaloosa, AL 35487-0001
Web site: bama.ua.edu/~exd
Email: info@exd.ccs.ua.edu
Phone: (205) 348 3019
Year founded: 1831
Ownership: Nonprofit, state
Accreditation: Regional (Southern Association of Colleges and Schools)
Residency: Three-day introductory seminar
Cost: $$$

Students 23 and older can design an individualized B.A. or B.S. with emphasis in an education-related field. With the exception of one 3-day planning seminar on campus at the beginning of the program, all learning can take place at a distance through online classes, correspondence courses, telecourses, intensive courses, and contract learning. Credit is awarded for prior study at regionally accredited universities, equivalency exams, and life-experience assessment. A senior project is required.

UNIVERSITY OF ILLINOIS AT SPRINGFIELD

Liberal Studies Online - BRK 427
P.O. Box 19243
Springfield, IL 62794
Web site: lis.uis.edu
Email: lis@uis.edu
Phone: (217) 206 6962 • (800) 323 9243
Fax: (217) 206 6217
Year founded: 1969
Ownership: Nonprofit, state
Accreditation: Regional (North Central Association of Colleges and Schools)
Residency: None
Cost: $$$

Offers an online B.S. completion program in liberal studies that can be tailored to meet the specific interests of each student. Up to 76 semester hours (60 lower-level, 16 upper-level) may be transferred into the program, and more credit may be awarded on the basis of standardized examinations or life-experience assessment. At least 30 semester hours must be earned online through UIS.

UNIVERSITY OF IOWA

Division of Continuing Education
116 International Center
Iowa City, IA 52242-1802
Web site: www.uiowa.edu
Email: credit-programs@uiowa.edu
Phone: (319) 335 2575 • (800) 272 6430
Fax: (319) 335 2740
Year founded: 1847
Ownership: Nonprofit, state
Accreditation: Regional (North Central Association of Colleges and Schools)
Residency: None
Cost: $$$

Offers an online Bachelor of Liberal Studies (B.L.S.) in cooperation with Pennsylvania State University through the "LionHawk" program. Students complete an A.A. in liberal studies through Penn State, and are automatically accepted into the Iowa B.L.S. completion program. Students who have already earned an associate's degree or the equivalent amount of credit may apply directly to the B.L.S. completion program. The program can be completed entirely through online study.

UNIVERSITY OF SOUTH FLORIDA

4202 East Fowler Avenue
Tampa, FL 33620
Web site: www.cas.usf.edu/bis
Email: issdept@nosferatu.cas.usf.edu

Phone: (813) 974 4058
Fax: (813) 974 5101
Year founded: 1956
Ownership: Nonprofit, state
Accreditation: Regional (Southern Association
of Colleges and Schools)
Residency: Four to six weeks total, spread
out over several summers
Cost: $$$

Offers a Bachelor of Independent Studies (B.I.S.) almost entirely by distance learning, with a cumulative four to six weeks worth of residential summer intensives. A good bit of transfer credit is accepted, and some credit is awarded by examination and for prior learning. The average student takes about five years to complete the program.

UNIVERSITY OF WISCONSIN—GREEN BAY

2420 Nicolet Drive
Green Bay, WI 54311-7001
Web site: www.wisc.edu
Phone: (608) 262 1234
Fax: (608) 262 0123
Year founded: 1978
Ownership: Nonprofit, state
Accreditation: Regional (North Central
Association of Colleges and Schools)
Residency: Two Saturday workshops
Cost: $$$

B.A. in interdisciplinary studies through online study, correspondence coursework, and prior learning (transfer credit, credit by examination, and life-experience assessment). Alternate modes of instruction include radio, telecourses, and internships. Two Saturday workshops on-campus are required.

UNIVERSITY OF WISCONSIN—SUPERIOR

Extended Degree Program
Erlanson 105
P.O. Box 2000
Superior, WI 54880
Web site: edp.uwsuper.edu
Email: extdegree@uwsuperior.edu
Phone: (715) 394 8487
Fax: (715) 394 8139
Year founded: 1893
Ownership: Nonprofit, state
Accreditation: Regional (North Central
Association of Colleges and Schools)
Residency: Negotiable
Cost: $$$

Offers an individualized B.S. entirely through off-campus study (online courses, correspondence courses, and contract learning); on-campus conferences with faculty members may be required. Transfer credit is accepted, and credit may be awarded on the basis of a prior learning evaluation.

WESTERN ILLINOIS UNIVERSITY

Non-Traditional Programs
5 Horrabin Hall
1 University Circle
Macomb, IL 61455
Web site: www.wiu.edu/users/mintp
Email: np-bot@wiu.edu
Phone: (309) 298 1929
Fax: (309) 298 2226
Year founded: 1899
Ownership: Nonprofit, state
Accreditation: Regional (North Central
Association of Colleges and Schools)
Residency: None
Cost: $$$

The Board of Trustees B.A. is an individualized program that can be completed entirely by distance learning; credit is awarded for transferred coursework, proficiency examinations, and prior learning assessment. At least 15 semester hours must be earned through WIU. Online, correspondence, and extension-based courses are available.

CHAPTER 3

Earning a Teaching Credential by Distance Learning

Are you he who would assume a place to teach, or be a poet here in The States?
The place is august—the terms obdurate.
Who would assume to teach here, may well prepare himself, body and mind,
He may well survey, ponder, arm, fortify, harden, make lithe, himself,
He shall surely be question'd beforehand by me with many and stern questions.

WALT WHITMAN

To teach in a public school (K–12), most states in the U.S. require that you have a license, not unlike a license required to practice in such professions as law or medicine. This license is most widely known as a teaching "credential," although some states refer to it as a certificate or—calling it like it is—a license. (In this book, we'll stick to "credential" for general use.)

Although the teaching credential is issued by the state, the coursework is provided by public and private universities. Some people earn their credential through education-focused bachelor's programs (described in the last chapter). Most people, however, decide to enter the teaching profession with a bachelor's degree already under their belt, and must therefore earn their teaching credential independently of undergraduate work, either through a dedicated credential program or as part of a master's. In this chapter, we look at distance-learning options for the post-bachelor's route.

Note: Although private schools are not legally bound to hire credentialed teachers, more and more of them want or demand that their teachers meet state licensure requirements. If only in the interest of job flexibility, it's a good idea for a private school teacher to get credentialed if he is committed to teaching as a long-term career.

What is required to get a teaching credential

For 50 states there are 50 different sets of requirements. The fact that the piece of paper that qualifies you to teach is called different things in different states makes it all even more complicated. As noted above, teaching credentials, certificates, and licenses are usually the same thing—but even this can vary. Bowing to the need to hire teachers when no fully qualified applicants are available, Hawaii, for example, has both a credential and a license, the former serving as an interim step towards the latter.

Then there are different kinds of credentials for teaching at different grade levels.

A single-subject credential testifies to the fact that you have sufficient knowledge in one specific area to teach that subject to others. Examples of this might be history or English. A multiple-subjects credential prepares you to teach in the self-enclosed classroom. Primarily this is the credential used for elementary school teachers.

Though it's hard to generalize about teacher credentialing, we're going to give it a shot. Bear in mind, however, that every state has the right to decide what constitutes appropriate training and education for their teachers. Common state licensure requirements include:

1. **A bachelor's degree**, in an academic subject (such as history, English, or math) for those seeking single-subject certification, or in liberal studies or elementary education for those seeking multiple-subjects certification.

2. **Completion of a teacher preparation program**. Usually this involves coursework, as well as some sort of apprentice program, often called "student teaching," that gets you in the classroom in front of students. Some states require the master's degree (or the master's degree within a specified number of years after you've started teaching).

3. **Completion of some variety of competency test**. Some of the assessments test basic literacy (such as California's CBEST) while others test subject matter competence (such as the MSAT used by many states to assess basic subject knowledge for elementary teachers).

We can hear some of you gulping right now. "I didn't know I wanted to teach second grade when I went to college! I don't have a degree in elementary education; I majored in French literature." Or "I have a degree in history (where there are few teaching jobs) and I would like to teach math (where there are lots of jobs). Does this mean I have to go back to college and get a B.A. in mathematics?"

No, it doesn't. There are several ways around this (ask your specific state for details). The most common would be "testing out" of the subject knowledge. For elementary school teachers, many states will accept, in lieu of a degree in elementary education, a passing score on the Multiple Subjects Assessment for Teachers (MSAT) administered by the Educational Testing Service (ETS). The MSAT consists of a multiple-choice Content Knowledge Section (two hours) and a constructed-response Content Area Exercises Section (three hours). It's certainly not a walk in the park, but it is a way to side-step additional coursework.

There are also single-subject assessments for those who wish to "test out" of a major. Depending on your state, taking the single-subject assessment in, for example, math could qualify you to teach it at the secondary level. One caveat: There are many variations of these tests (for example, six different biology assessments and five different math assessments). Which particular ones (and you may likely need to take more than one) is left up to your state licensing office to determine.

Information on both of these assessments is available from:

EDUCATIONAL TESTING SERVICE
Teaching and Learning Division
Rosedale Road
Princeton, NJ 08541
Email: praxis@ets.org
Phone: (609) 771 7395

Finding out your state's specific requirements

Okay, now that we've given you the sweeping generalizations, it's time for you to figure out the specific requirements for your state.

First, contact your state's teacher licensing department. We've compiled the contact information for all 50 offices at the back of this book in Appendix A.

Next, get in touch with your county office of education and/or your local school district(s) and get their lowdown. Don't be surprised if any of these bureaucracies disagree with each other. Decide who has the most power (usually the teacher licensing department), and go from there.

Choosing a credential program

Here are some guidelines for making sure that your program meets your needs:

► Make sure that the program has regional accreditation, which, almost without exception, is required for employment in the public schools and/or for teacher licensure. For the whole story on the importance of accreditation and how to check up on it, see Appendix C (starting on page 113).

► Beyond regional accreditation, a teacher preparation program should also be approved by the National Council for Accreditation of Teacher Education (NCATE) (*www.ncate.org*). With few exceptions, this is required for state licensure. In addition, it provides a minimum level of quality assurance.

► Check that the credential program is on your state's approved list. Better to be safe than sorry.

► Make sure you're getting the right kind of credential for the grade level you want to teach. In general, a single-subject credential qualifies you to teach a specific subject in the middle or high school classroom; the multiple-subjects credential is for elementary school teachers

Credential Programs by Distance Learning

As evidenced below, not very many credential programs are being offered through distance learning. Most of these programs did not even exist three years ago. Student-teaching makes distance learning in this field difficult. It's easy enough to complete credential coursework by distance methods, but many states require apprenticeship in the classroom. For example, National University makes it possible to do all of the credential courses online, except for the student-teaching component. This is a common model.

We've divided these listings into two groups: credential-only programs and programs that combine a credential with a master's degree. All the programs listed are regionally accredited and approved by the National Council for Accreditation of Teacher Education (NCATE). Programs are organized by U.S. state. Don't see your state listed? Go to the sidebar on page 35 for advice on how to transfer a credential from one state to another.

If you do not find the program you seek, please do not attack the Bear.

Credential-Only Programs

Alabama

UNIVERSITY OF SOUTH ALABAMA

Office of Admissions
182 Administrative Building
Mobile, AL 36688-0002
Web site: usaonline.southalabama.edu
Email: admiss@usamail.usouthal.edu
Phone: (334) 460 6141 • (800) 872 5247
Fax: (334) 460 7876
Year founded: 1963
Ownership: Nonprofit, state
Accreditation: Regional (Southern Association
of Colleges and Schools)
Residency: None, generally
Cost: $$$
Special fields: Collaborative teacher education,
gifted education

Graduate certificates in the above fields, designed
to meet Alabama's Class A teaching certification
requirements.

Alaska

UNIVERSITY OF ALASKA

1120 Glacier Highway
Juneau, AK 99801
Web site: www.uas.alaska.edu/uas/
brochure_NET.shtml
Email: jyuas@uas.alaska.edu
Phone: (907) 465 6457 • (877) 465 4827
Fax: (907) 465 6365
Year founded: 1917
Ownership: Nonprofit, state
Accreditation: Regional (Northwest
Association of Schools and Colleges)
Residency: None
Cost: $$$

Online Alaska Type A teacher certification program.

Arizona

PRESCOTT COLLEGE

220 Grove Avenue
Prescott, AZ 86301
Web site: www.prescott.edu
Email: admissions@prescott.edu
Phone: (520) 778 2090 • (800) 628 6364
Year founded: 1966
Ownership: Nonprofit, independent
Accreditation: Regional (North Central
Association of Colleges and Schools)

Residency: One 3-day colloquium per semester
Cost: $$$$

Offers a low-residency certification program for
Arizona teachers.

California

CALIFORNIA STATE UNIVERSITY—
CALSTATETEACH PROGRAM

Teacher Preparation Program
Student Services
401 Golden Shore
Long Beach, CA 90802
Web site: www.calstateteach.net
Phone: (877) 225 7828
Ownership: Nonprofit, state
Accreditation: Regional (Western Association
of Schools and Colleges)
Residency: None

Cost: $$

Offers an online credential program for California intern teachers who have already secured a K–8 teaching position within the state. Not available for out-of-state teachers. Its primary purpose is to serve elementary school teachers who do not possess a teaching credential.

CALIFORNIA STATE UNIVERSITY—FRESNO

AIC - Distance Learning
5241 N. Maple Avenue
McKee Fisk Building, Room 110
Fresno, CA 93740-8027
Web site: www.csufresno.edu/aic/
 distance.html
Phone: (559) 278 2058
Fax: (559) 278 7026
Year founded: 1911
Ownership: Nonprofit, state
Accreditation: Regional (Western Association
 of Schools and Colleges)
Residency: None
Cost: $$
Special fields: Applied linguistics/TESOL

Multiple-subject CLAD (Cross-Cultural Linguistic Academic Development) credential/certificate through off-campus study. Instruction is given through televised classes at various sites in the San Joaquin Valley of California.

CALIFORNIA STATE UNIVERSITY—HAYWARD

Extended and Continuing Education
25800 Carlos Bee Boulevard
Hayward, CA 94542-3012
Web site: www.online.csuhayward.edu
Email: online@csuhayward.edu
Phone: (510) 885 3605
Fax: (510) 885 4817
Year founded: 1957
Ownership: Nonprofit, state
Accreditation: Regional (Western Association
 of Schools and Colleges)
Residency: None
Cost: $$
Special fields: Spanish, online teaching & learning

Offers an online CLAD (Cross-Cultural Linguistic Academic Development) certificate in Spanish for teachers, as well as an online certificate in online teaching and learning.

NATIONAL UNIVERSITY

11255 North Torrey Pines Road
La Jolla, CA 92037-1011
Web site: www.nu.edu

Email: getinfo@nu.edu
Phone: (619) 563 7100 • (800) 628 8648
Fax: (619) 642 8714
Year founded: 1971
Ownership: Nonprofit, independent
Accreditation: Regional (Western Association
 of Schools and Colleges)
Residency: None for coursework, but student
 teaching required
Cost: $$$

Offers a low-residency California teacher certification program.

Florida

NOVA SOUTHEASTERN UNIVERSITY

3301 College Avenue
Fort Lauderdale, FL 33314
Web site: www.nova.edu
Email: cwis@nova.edu
Phone: (954) 262 8500 • (800) 541 6682
Year founded: 1964
Ownership: Nonprofit, independent
Accreditation: Regional (Southern Association
 of Colleges and Schools)
Residency: Monthly four-day seminars
Cost: $$$

Offers a variety of online certificate programs, including a credential program under review by the Florida Department of Education as a possible teaching credential.

Maine

ST. JOSEPH'S COLLEGE

278 White's Bridge Road
Standish, ME 04084-5263
Web site: www.sjcme.edu/cps
Email: admiss@sjcme.edu
Phone: (800) 752 4723
Year founded: 1912
Ownership: Nonprofit
Accreditation: Regional (New England
 Association of Schools and Colleges)
Residency: None
Cost: $$$

Certificate in teaching designed to meet Maine teacher licensure requirements.

Virginia

REGENT UNIVERSITY

Graduate Center
1650 Diagonal Road
Alexandria, VA 22314-2857

No distance-learning credential program in your state?

Unfortunately, too many states are without credential programs that can be earned by distance learning. But here's a possible way around this. Go ahead and earn a credential from another state's distance-learning program, after having checked that the program has reciprocity with your state. Reciprocity means that a state accepts as valid a teaching credential from another state. This is negotiated on a state-by-state basis.

If reciprocity exists, after earning a credential in another state, usually you will only have to complete an extra course or two to satisfy requirements in your home state, and the kicker is that most states will let you start teaching before you finish those extra courses.

The only problem might be the student teaching component. If the credential program you've chosen requires one, you may need to go to the other state. However, the "foreign" university might be able to work out an agreement with a school district local to you. Ask. Nothing ventured, nothing gained. However, even if you do have to go to that other state, better 3 or 4 months than 18.

Following is a list of all of the states which have signed the Interstate Agreement on Qualification of Educational Personnel. In theory, these states will have reciprocity with each other. However, public education being what it is, it's not quite as neat as that. Some additional courses will likely be required; how many depends on your state. Also, some of the states are signatories in name only, but don't quite honor the letter of the agreement.

Talk about a strict supervising teacher . . . !

Alabama	Georgia	Maryland	New Mexico	South Carolina
Arkansas	Hawaii	Massachusetts	North Carolina	Tennessee
California	Idaho	Michigan	Ohio	Texas
Colorado	Illinois	Mississippi	Oklahoma	Utah
Connecticut	Indiana	Montana	Oregon	Vermont
Delaware	Kentucky	Nevada	Pennsylvania	Virginia
District of Columbia	Louisiana	New Hampshire	Puerto Rico	Washington
Florida	Maine	New Jersey	Rhode Island	West Virginia

Web site: www.regent.edu
Email: admissions@regent.edu
Phone: (757) 226 4127 • (800) 373 5504
Fax: (703) 740 1471
Year founded: 1977
Ownership: Nonprofit, independent
Accreditation: Regional (Southern Association of Colleges and Schools)
Residency: Variable
Cost: $$$$

The low-residency credential program is designed to meet Virginia state teaching licensure requirements.

Credential-Track Master's Programs

Some states require, if you did not complete an approved program for teacher education and licensure as an undergraduate, that you complete these requirements through a credential-track master's program. And even if a master's degree is not required, you may be attracted to the higher salary that it commands in most states. Below are programs that combine a credential with a master's degree.

Alabama

UNIVERSITY OF SOUTH ALABAMA

Office of Admissions
182 Administrative Building
Mobile, AL 36688-0002
Web site: usaonline.southalabama.edu
Email: admiss@usamail.usouthal.edu
Phone: (334) 460 6141 • (800) 872 5247
Fax: (334) 460 7876
Year founded: 1963
Ownership: Nonprofit, state
Accreditation: Regional (Southern Association of Colleges and Schools)
Residency: Variable
Cost: $$$
Special fields: Collaborative teacher education, gifted education

M.Ed.'s in the above fields are designed to meet Alabama's Class A teaching certification requirements. Coursework can be completed online, but students seeking Class A certification may be required to attend some short residency sessions.

Maryland

UNIVERSITY OF MARYLAND

University College
3501 University Boulevard, East
Adelphi, MD 20783
Web site: www.umuc.edu
Email: umucinfo@umuc.edu
Phone: (301) 985 7000 • (800) 888 8682
Fax: (301) 454 0399
Year founded: 1856
Ownership: Nonprofit, state
Accreditation: Regional (Middle States Association of Colleges and Schools)
Residency: None
Cost: $$$

The Master of Arts in Teaching (M.A.T.) meets Maryland state licensure requirements for basic teacher certification; the curriculum consists of nine courses and a capstone internship with seminar.

Virginia

LIBERTY UNIVERSITY

1971 University Boulevard
Lynchburg, VA 24502-2269
Web site: www.liberty.edu
Email: admissions@liberty.edu
Phone: (804) 582 2000 • (800) 424 9595
Fax: (804) 582 2304
Year founded: 1971
Ownership: Nonprofit, independent
Accreditation: Regional (Southern Association of Colleges and Schools)
Residency: Variable
Cost: $$$$
Special fields: Administration & supervision, elementary education, general education, reading specialist, school counseling, secondary education, special education

Offers a low-residency M.Ed. in the fields listed above; all programs are designed to meet Virginia state licensure requirements. Students are required to complete four core courses, four concentration courses (seven for the school counseling concentration), and four professional courses (five for students seeking Virginia state teaching licensure). No thesis is required. All students seeking Virginia state licensure must take at least nine hours of residential coursework (although this coursework is available in a special intensive format and can be completed during summer residencies).

CHAPTER 4

Earning a Master's in Education by Distance Learning

Teachers will not come to the school knowing all they have to know, but knowing how to figure out what they need to know, where to get it, and how to help others make meaning out of it.

CARNEGIE CORPORATION OF NEW YORK

For the career educator, a master's degree is a no-brainer. Getting one can sharpen your skills, boost your salary, focus your expertise, and open doors to career advancement. Some of the reasons you might want a master's include:

▶ **A higher salary.** In most school districts, having a master's automatically moves you up the salary scale, worth up to several thousand dollars per year. In some states (such as Washington and Mississippi), you can't move up the scale until you have the higher degree. California rewards not the master's degree itself but the units you earned to get there.

▶ **Meeting state requirements.** Some states (such as New York and Massachusetts) require working teachers to earn a master's degree within five years of initial licensure.

▶ **Specializing.** A master's degree can be highly useful for a teacher who wants to move into a specialized field, such as guidance counseling or special education.

▶ **A desire to administer.** Where a master's is not explicitly required for an administrative job, it might as well be: If you don't have one, the other person competing for the job will.

▶ **Doctoral goals.** If you're aiming for a Ph.D. or Ed.D. down the line, a master's is almost always a required step along the way.

"Well, okay, how about this: your M.S. in molecular biology for my M.A. in history and a postgraduate diploma to be named later."

Schools Offering Education-Related Master's Programs by Distance Learning

You'll notice that this chapter has more programs than any of the other chapters. The focused yet flexible nature of master's-level work seems to lend itself well to distance learning. And distance learning, in turn, lends itself well to the typical master's degree candidate: a mature, working teacher with plenty of personal obligations to juggle. The programs listed below make it much easier to earn a master's without having to break stride for your work or personal life.

The listings are organized by kind of degree: first, master's in general education; then specialized master's programs by category.

Credential-Track Master's Degrees

Included in this chapter are three programs—offered by Liberty University, University of Maryland, and University of South Alabama— that combine a master's with a state credential, designed for those who hold a bachelor's degree but are not yet licensed teachers. For more information on this strategy and these programs, see chapter 3.

". . . though profoundly intersubjective, our pedagogical methodology can be delineated to represent a uniquely dichotomous—" Oh, bother. Page 397, and I still haven't gotten to that sex scene everybody's been telling me about.

Key to listings

NAME OF SCHOOL
Postal Address *(United States if country not specified)*
Web site URL
Email address
Phone • Tollfree phone *(If a U.S. number, country code (+1) not included)*
Fax
Year founded
Ownership Proprietary or nonprofit (state, independent, or church)
Accreditation Type of accreditation (regional, national, or non-U.S. equivalent) and responsible agency. All schools listed in this book have proper accreditation. See Appendix C for a more thorough explanation of this concept.
Residency Amount of on-campus attendance required
Cost Subjective interpretation of school's relative cost: $ (dirt cheap) to $$$$$ (expensive)
Special fields Fields of study, if other than general education
Description Specific information on the school's offerings

Education (general)

CAPELLA UNIVERSITY
222 South 9th Street, 20th Floor
Minneapolis, MN 55402-3389
Web site: www.capellauniversity.edu
Email: info@capella.edu
Phone: (612) 339 8650 • (888) 227 3552
Fax: (612) 337 5396
Year founded: 1993
Ownership: Proprietary
Accreditation: Regional (North Central Association of Colleges and Schools)
Residency: None
Cost: $$$$
Offers an M.S. in education. Students may choose a general track (consisting of six core courses and six

elective courses) or from a selection of more specialized tracks (described in later sections below). A capstone project is required. All coursework may be completed online.

CENTRAL QUEENSLAND UNIVERSITY
Bruce Highway
Rockhampton, Qld 4702
Australia
Web site: www.dflc.cqu.edu.au
Email: ddce-enquiries@cqu.edu.au
Phone: +61 (7) 4930 9719
Fax: +61 (7) 4930 9792
Year founded: 1967
Ownership: Nonprofit
Accreditation: Non-U.S. equivalent
Residency: None
Cost: $$
The Master of Education Studies involves eight elective course modules. Students choose coursework from fields such as education law, school personnel management, and curriculum design, and may design independent study or supervised reading courses with faculty approval. No thesis is required, and the program can be completed entirely by distance learning.

CHARLES STURT UNIVERSITY
International Division
Locked Bag 676
Wagga Wagga, New South Wales 2678
Australia
Web site: www.csu.edu.au
Email: inquiry@csu.edu.au
Phone: +61 (2) 6933 2666
Fax: +61 (2) 6933 2799
Year founded: 1989
Ownership: Nonprofit
Accreditation: Non-U.S. equivalent
Residency: None
Cost: $$
The M.Ed. is available with a coursework-only track (consisting of eight course modules) and a coursework-with-project track (consisting of six modules and a capstone project). It is possible to complete either track in about two years of part-time study. No residency is required.

COLLEGE OF ST. SCHOLASTICA
Master of Education Department
1200 Kenwood Avenue
Duluth, MN 55811
Web site: www.css.edu
Email: admissions@css.edu

Phone: (218) 723 6000 • (800) 888 8796
Fax: (218) 723 5991
Year founded: 1912
Ownership: Nonprofit, church
Accreditation: Regional (North Central
   Association of Colleges and Schools)
Residency: Two weekend seminars
Cost: $$$$

Offers an M.Ed. almost entirely through online study; the only required residencies are two weekend seminars on reflective practice and professional reflection (derived from the school's strong Benedictine tradition). The 32-semester-hour curriculum consists of an 18-hour core, 8 hours of field electives, and 6 hours of general electives (which need not be in education, and can be transferred in from another regionally accredited institution).

CONCORDIA UNIVERSITY

275 Syndicate Street North
St. Paul, MN 55104
Web site: www.csp.edu/hspd
Email: cshs@csp.edu
Phone: (651) 641 8897 • (800) 211 3370
Fax: (651) 603 6144
Year founded: 1893
Ownership: Nonprofit, church
Accreditation: Regional (Middle States
   Association of Colleges and Schools)
Residency: One initial five-day residency
Cost: $$$

Offers M.A. programs in education with emphasis in early childhood, parish education and administration, school-age care, or youth development. Students must attend an initial five-day residency, but all other work may be completed online. The program concludes with a capstone seminar (which must be a thesis, an appropriate portfolio, or another approved project).

DEAKIN UNIVERSITY

Deakin International
336 Glenferrie Road
Malvern, Victoria 3144
Australia
Web site: www.deakin.edu.au
Phone: +61 (3) 9244 5095
Fax: +61 (3) 9244 5094
Year founded: 1974
Ownership: Nonprofit
Accreditation: Non-U.S. equivalent
Residency: None
Cost: $$

Offers a Master of Education through correspondence, online study, and/or a mix of the two. The program takes two to three years to complete. Students may choose a coursework-only track or a coursework-and-research track.

EDITH COWAN UNIVERSITY

International Students Office
Claremont, West Australia 6010
Australia
Web site: www.cowan.edu.au
Email: extstudi@echidna.cowan.edu.au
Phone: +61 (9) 273 8681
Year founded: 1990
Ownership: Nonprofit
Accreditation: Non-U.S. equivalent
Residency: None
Cost: $$

Offers an M.Ed. externally, with optional specializations in a vast array of fields. Students may choose a coursework-only track (comprised of eight course modules), a coursework-and-project track (comprised of six course modules and a capstone project), or a coursework-and-thesis track (comprised of four course modules and a thesis). Takes two to five years to complete. No residency is required.

LIBERTY UNIVERSITY

1971 University Boulevard
Lynchburg, VA 24502-2269
Web site: www.liberty.edu
Email: admissions@liberty.edu
Phone: (804) 582 2000 • (800) 424 9595
Fax: (804) 582 2304
Year founded: 1971
Ownership: Nonprofit, independent
Accreditation: Regional (Southern Association
   of Colleges and Schools)
Residency: Variable
Cost: $$$$

Offers a low-residency Master of Education (M.Ed.), designed to meet Virginia state licensure requirements. Students are required to complete four core courses, four concentration courses, and four professional courses (five for students seeking Virginia state teaching licensure). No thesis is required. Students may be required to take some coursework in residence; in particular, all students seeking Virginia state licensure must take at least nine hours of residential coursework (though this coursework is available in a special intensive format and can be completed during summer residencies).

MONASH UNIVERSITY

Distance Education Centre
Gippsland Campus
Northways Road
Churchill, Victoria 3842
Australia
Web site: www.monash.edu.au/de
Email: course.inquiries@celts.monash.edu.au
Phone: +61 (3) 9902 6200
Fax: +61 (3) 9902 6300
Year founded: 1961
Ownership: Nonprofit
Accreditation: Non-U.S. equivalent
Residency: None
Cost: $$

The M.Ed. is available with three tracks: coursework-only (consisting of six course modules), coursework-and-paper (consisting of five modules and a short thesis of 10,000 words), or coursework-and-thesis (consisting of four modules and a thesis of 20,000 words). Coursework takes place primarily via correspondence (supplemented in some cases with audiocassettes); an increasing number of courses are also available online.

OPEN UNIVERSITY

Walton Hall
Milton Keynes MK7 6AA
United Kingdom
Web site: www.open.ac.uk
Email: ces-gen@open.ac.uk
Phone: +44 (190) 827 4066
Fax: +44 (190) 865 3744
Year founded: 1969
Ownership: Nonprofit
Accreditation: Non-U.S. equivalent
Residency: None
Cost: $$

The M.A. in education consists of three extraordinarily intensive course modules; students may choose a general individualized program or specialize in applied linguistics, lifelong learning management, or special needs and inclusive education. All coursework can be completed by correspondence, and no thesis is required.

PRESCOTT COLLEGE

220 Grove Avenue
Prescott, AZ 86301
Web site: www.prescott.edu
Email: admissions@prescott.edu
Phone: (520) 778 2090 • (800) 628 6364
Year founded: 1966
Ownership: Nonprofit, independent
Accreditation: Regional (North Central
   Association of Colleges and Schools)
Residency: One 3-day colloquium per semester
Cost: $$$$

Offers an individualized M.A. program in education. Students design learning contracts with faculty assistance, and the program can incorporate field work, internships, and the like. A capstone thesis or project is required.

REGENT UNIVERSITY

Graduate Center
1650 Diagonal Road
Alexandria, VA 22314-2857
Web site: www.regent.edu
Email: admissions@regent.edu
Phone: (757) 226 4127 • (800) 373 5504
Fax: (703) 740 1471
Year founded: 1977
Ownership: Nonprofit, independent
Accreditation: Regional (Southern Association
   of Colleges and Schools)
Residency: None
Cost: $$$$

Regent University offers an individualized online M.Ed. program. Students complete 10 online courses (taken from a wide selection, including a number of courses designed specifically for Christian school educators) and a capstone project. All requirements may be completed via online study.

ST. JOSEPH'S COLLEGE

278 White's Bridge Road
Standish, ME 04084-5263
Web site: www.sjcme.edu/cps
Email: admiss@sjcme.edu
Phone: (800) 752 4723
Year founded: 1912
Ownership: Nonprofit
Accreditation: Regional (New England
   Association of Schools and Colleges)
Residency: One 2-week session
Cost: $$$

The M.S. in education, with emphasis in teaching and learning, explores reflective practice, lifelong learning, and a cross-section of other issues, many of them not often addressed in a program of this kind. Students complete five core courses, five elective courses, and a capstone thesis or project.

SOUTH BANK UNIVERSITY

103 Borough Road
London SE1 0AA
United Kingdom
Web site: www.southbank-university.ac.uk
Email: internat@sbu.ac.uk
Phone: +44 (20) 7815 6137
Fax: +44 (20) 7815 6199
Ownership: Nonprofit
Accreditation: Non-U.S. equivalent
Residency: Six weeks per year (negotiable)
Cost: $$$

Students worldwide may apply to South Bank's research-based M.Phil. program in education. Although most students are expected to spend six weeks on campus per year, the school may be willing to negotiate with students who are unable to meet this requirement.

UNIVERSITY OF BRADFORD

Student Registry, Postgraduate
Richmond Road
Bradford BD7 1DP
United Kingdom
Web site: www.brad.ac.uk
Email: pg-admissions@bradford.ac.uk
Phone: +44 (1274) 233 042
Fax: +44 (1274) 235 810
Year founded: 1957
Ownership: Nonprofit
Accreditation: Non-U.S. equivalent
Residency: Two weeks per year
Cost: $$$

Offers a research-based M.Phil. in education, with two weeks of on-campus residency per year. Likely duration: two to five years.

While many M.Ed. programs have online exams, sometimes an in-person examination is required.

UNIVERSITY OF MELBOURNE

Victoria, 3010
Australia
Web site: www.unimelb.edu.au/research
Email: j.gilbert@sgs.unimelb.edu.au
Phone: +61 (3) 8344 8670
Ownership: Nonprofit
Accreditation: Non-U.S. equivalent
Residency: Negotiable
Cost: $$

One of the most prestigious research universities in Australia, Melbourne makes its research M.Phil. program in education available to students worldwide who are able to find, and work through, an approved local institution (the list of approved institutions is already fairly extensive, and students may petition to have new institutions added to the list). The program involves two to five years of study and a dissertation of about 60,000 words.

UNIVERSITY OF NORTHERN IOWA

1227 West 27th Street
Cedar Falls, IA 50614
Web site: www.uni.edu
Email: contined@uni.edu
Phone: (319) 273 2121 • (800) 772 1746
Year founded: 1847
Ownership: Nonprofit, state
Accreditation: Regional (North Central Association of Colleges and Schools)
Residency: Regional workshops and on-campus summer intensives
Cost: $$$

Offers an M.A. in education (with optional specialization in educational leadership, elementary reading and language arts, middle school education, middle school mathematics, or special education and inclusion) through a combination of online study, regional extension workshops, and summer intensive seminars.

UNIVERSITY OF PRETORIA

Pretoria 0002
South Africa
Web site: www.up.ac.za/telematic
Email: telehelp@postino.up.ac.za
Phone: +27 (12) 420 3884
Fax: +27 (12) 362 5168
Year founded: 1930
Ownership: Nonprofit
Accreditation: Non-U.S. equivalent
Residency: Variable
Cost: $$

Offers a general M.Ed. through a mix of correspondence, Web-based, and on-campus study. Also has programs in computer-assisted education, education management, music education, and potential development in education and training (listed in their respective sections below).

UNIVERSITY OF SARASOTA

5250 17th Street
Sarasota, FL 34235
Web site: www.sarasota.edu
Email: uofs@embanet.com
Phone: (941) 379 0404 • (800) 331 5995
Fax: (941) 379 9464
Year founded: 1969
Ownership: Proprietary
Accreditation: Regional (Southern Association of Colleges and Schools)
Residency: One weekend per month for two months
Cost: $$$$

For the M.A. in education, students complete seven courses by distance learning (online and/or correspondence) and six courses "in-residence" (meeting one weekend per month for 2 months, with remaining work taking place by distance learning). The program can be completed in as little as 13 months. We've heard reports that the University of Sarasota may change its name to Argosy University (the school is owned by the Argosy Education Group), but the matter was still not settled when we went to press.

UNIVERSITY OF SOUTH AFRICA

P.O. Box 392
Unisa 0003
South Africa
Web site: www.unisa.ac.za
Email: study-info@unisa.ac.za
Phone: +27 (12) 429 3111
Fax: +27 (12) 429 3221
Year founded: 1873
Ownership: Nonprofit, state
Accreditation: Non-U.S. equivalent
Residency: None
Cost: $

Offers an M.Ed. with optional specialization in a number of fields. Students complete four to six intensive course modules and a thesis. All work can be completed by correspondence, though an increasing number of courses are also available online. No residency is required. UNISA has been stepping up efforts to attract U.S. students, and a correspondent tells us that UNISA may be seeking additional accreditation through the Distance Education and Training Council (DETC).

UNIVERSITY OF SOUTHERN QUEENSLAND

International Office
Toowoomba, Queensland 4350
Australia
Web site: www.usqonline.com.au
Email: international@usq.edu.au
Phone: +61 (7) 4631 2362
Fax: +61 (7) 4636 2211
Year founded: 1967
Ownership: Nonprofit
Accreditation: Non-U.S. equivalent
Residency: None
Cost: $$

The M.Ed. consists of eight modules and a capstone research project. Students may choose a general major (with the student's choice of courses), or specialize in educational technology, online education, or open and distance learning. All coursework may be completed online, and no residency is required.

UNIVERSITY OF TASMANIA

Board of Graduate Studies by Research
Churchill Avenue, Sandy Bay
G.P.O. Box 252-45
Hobart, Tasmania 7001
Australia
Web site: www.international.utas.edu.au
Email: international.office@utas.edu.au
Phone: +61 (3) 6226 2762
Fax: +61 (3) 6226 7497
Ownership: Nonprofit
Accreditation: Non-U.S. equivalent
Residency: Negotiable
Cost: $$

Offers an M.Phil. in education by research (two to five years of study culminating in a dissertation of about 60,000 words). Some on-campus residencies may be required.

UNIVERSITY OF WALES—ABERYSTWYTH

Old College, King Street
Aberystwyth, Ceredigion
Wales SY23 2AX
United Kingdom
Web site: www.aber.ac.uk
Email: rlw@aber.ac.uk
Phone: +44 (1970) 622 090
Fax: +44 (1970) 622 921

Year founded: 1872
Ownership: Nonprofit
Accreditation: Non-U.S. equivalent
Residency: Negotiable
Cost: $$$

Offers an M.Phil. in education by research. Students may work on the program part-time (traveling to Wales for yearly campus visits, generally of two to three weeks duration), or research full-time through a place of employment.

Administration and leadership

For those interested in becoming a public school administrator (vice-principal, principal, superintendent, et cetera), a master's degree, often in conjunction with an administrative credential, is required. The programs below may or may not meet the requirements for your state, so it would be wise to check first.

CAPELLA UNIVERSITY

222 South 9th Street, 20th Floor
Minneapolis, MN 55402-3389
Web site: www.capellauniversity.edu
Email: info@capella.edu
Phone: (612) 339 8650 • (888) 227 3552
Fax: (612) 337 5396
Year founded: 1993
Ownership: Proprietary
Accreditation: Regional (North Central Association of Colleges and Schools)
Residency: None
Cost: $$$$
Special fields: Educational administration

Offers an M.S. in education with emphasis in educational administration; students complete five core courses, four specialization courses, and three elective courses. A capstone project is required. All coursework may be completed online.

CENTRAL QUEENSLAND UNIVERSITY

Bruce Highway
Rockhampton, Queensland 4702
Australia
Web site: www.dflc.cqu.edu.au
Email: ddce-enquiries@cqu.edu.au
Phone: +61 (7) 4930 9719
Fax: +61 (7) 4930 9792
Year founded: 1967
Ownership: Nonprofit
Accreditation: Non-U.S. equivalent

Residency: None
Cost: $$
Special fields: School management

The Master of School Management requires eight course modules: six core modules (in fields such as education policy, legal aspects of school management, financial management, educational leadership, and school personnel management) and two elective modules. The entire program may be completed off-campus, and no thesis or project is required.

DEAKIN UNIVERSITY

Deakin International
336 Glenferrie Road
Malvern, Victoria 3144
Australia
Web site: www.deakin.edu.au
Phone: +61 (3) 9244 5095
Fax: +61 (3) 9244 5094
Year founded: 1974
Ownership: Nonprofit
Accreditation: Non-U.S. equivalent
Residency: None
Cost: $$
Special fields: Curriculum & administration studies

Offers an M.Ed. in curriculum and administration studies; students may choose a coursework-only track or a coursework-and-research track. The program takes two to three years to complete via part-time study.

EDITH COWAN UNIVERSITY

International Students Office
Claremont, Western Australia 6010
Australia
Web site: www.cowan.edu.au
Email: extstudi@echidna.cowan.edu.au
Phone: +61 (9) 273 8681
Year founded: 1990
Ownership: Nonprofit
Accreditation: Non-U.S. equivalent
Residency: None
Cost: $$
Special fields: Educational policy & administrative studies

Offers an M.Ed. in educational policy and administrative studies. Students may choose a coursework-only track (comprised of eight course modules), a coursework-and-project track (comprised of six course modules and a capstone project), or a coursework-and-thesis track (comprised of four course modules and a thesis). Takes two to five years to complete. No residency is required.

KEELE UNIVERSITY

Postgraduate Admissions and Recruiting Office
Department of Academic Affairs
Staffordshire ST5 5BG
United Kingdom
Web site: www.keele.ac.uk
Email: aaa12@admin.keele.ac.uk
Phone: +44 (17) 8258 4002
Fax: +44 (17) 8263 2343
Year founded: 1949
Ownership: Nonprofit
Accreditation: Non-U.S. equivalent
Residency: None
Cost: $$$
Special fields: Effective education & management

Offers an M.A. in effective education and management by correspondence, consisting of seven taught modules (three in teaching, three in management, one in research) and a capstone dissertation. No residency is required.

LAKEHEAD UNIVERSITY

Graduate Studies in Education
Faculty of Education
955 Oliver Road
Thunder Bay, ON P7B 5E1
Canada
Web site: www.lakeheadu.ca
Phone: +1 (807) 343 8054
Fax: +1 (807) 346 7771
Ownership: Nonprofit
Accreditation: Non-U.S. equivalent
Residency: None
Cost: $$$
Special fields: Educational administration

Offers an M.Ed. in educational administration via correspondence or online study. Students may choose a coursework-and-thesis track (consisting of two compulsory courses, three electives, a graduate seminar, and a thesis) or a coursework-and-project track (consisting of two compulsory courses, five electives, a graduate seminar, and a project).

LIBERTY UNIVERSITY

1971 University Boulevard
Lynchburg, VA 24502-2269
Web site: www.liberty.edu
Email: admissions@liberty.edu
Phone: (804) 582 2000 • (800) 424 9595
Fax: (804) 582 2304
Year founded: 1971
Ownership: Nonprofit, independent

When Running Late read that his final exam in the forestry education course would be "on a tree," little did he know . . .

Accreditation: Regional (Southern Association of Colleges and Schools)
Residency: Variable
Cost: $$$$
Special fields: Administration & supervision

Offers a low-residency M.Ed. in administration and supervision, designed to meet Virginia state licensure requirements. Students are required to complete four core courses, four concentration courses, and four professional courses. No thesis is required. Students may be required to take coursework in residence; in particular, all students seeking Virginia state licensure must take at least nine hours of residential coursework (though this coursework is available in a special intensive format and can be completed during summer residencies).

OPEN UNIVERSITY

Walton Hall
Milton Keynes MK7 6AA
United Kingdom
Web site: www.open.ac.uk
Email: ces-gen@open.ac.uk
Phone: +44 (190) 827 4066
Fax: +44 (190) 865 3744
Year founded: 1969
Ownership: Nonprofit
Accreditation: Non-U.S. equivalent
Residency: None
Cost: $$
Special fields: Education management

The M.A. in education with emphasis in management consists of three intensive course modules. All coursework can be completed by correspondence, and no thesis is required.

SETON HALL UNIVERSITY

400 South Orange Avenue
South Orange, NJ 07079-2697
Web site: www.setonworldwide.net
Email: setonworldwide@shu.edu
Phone: (973) 642 8500 • (888) 738 6699
Fax: (973) 761 9234
Year founded: 1874
Ownership: Nonprofit, church
Accreditation: Regional (Middle States
      Association of Colleges and Schools)
Residency: Three weekends on campus
Cost: $$$$
Special fields: Educational administration
      & supervision

Offers a low-residency M.A. in education with specialization in educational administration and supervision. This program fulfills New Jersey State Education Department requirements for "Supervisor" certification. Students complete degree requirements as part of a cohort of 25 students. The 36-semester-hour curriculum consists of six intensive course modules (each worth 6 hours of credit). Students must attend a weekend seminar at the beginning, middle, and end of the program; all other requirements are completed online.

UNIVERSITY OF LEICESTER

University Road
Leicester LE1 7RH
United Kingdom
Web site: www.le.ac.uk
Email: higherdegrees@le.ac.uk
Phone: +44 (11) 6252 2298
Fax: +44 (11) 6252 2200
Year founded: 1921
Ownership: Nonprofit
Accreditation: Non-U.S. equivalent
Residency: None
Cost: $$$
Special fields: Education management

The MBA in educational management is open to teachers with at least three years of experience. The curriculum consists of five intensive course modules (emphasizing interdisciplinary approaches to the fields of management and educational leadership), and a management study (a thesis with practical elements) of at least 20,000 words. No on-campus residency is required.

UNIVERSITY OF NORTHERN IOWA

1227 West 27th Street
Cedar Falls, IA 50614
Web site: www.uni.edu
Email: contined@uni.edu
Phone: (319) 273 2121 • (800) 772 1746
Year founded: 1847
Ownership: Nonprofit, state
Accreditation: Regional (North Central
      Association of Colleges and Schools)
Residency: Regional classroom meetings and
      on-campus summer intensives
Cost: $$$
Special fields: Educational leadership

Offered through a mix of online study, regional extension workshops, and summer intensive seminars, the M.A. in education with emphasis in educational leadership is designed to fulfill Iowa state principal licensure requirements.

UNIVERSITY OF PRETORIA

Pretoria 0002
South Africa
Web site: www.up.ac.za/telematic
Email: telehelp@postino.up.ac.za
Phone: +27 (12) 420 3884
Fax: +27 (12) 362 5168
Year founded: 1930
Ownership: Nonprofit
Accreditation: Non-U.S. equivalent
Residency: Variable
Cost: $$
Special fields: Education management

The M.Ed. in education management can be completed through a mix of correspondence, Web-based, and on-campus study.

UNIVERSITY OF SOUTH AFRICA

P.O. Box 392
Unisa 0003
South Africa
Web site: www.unisa.ac.za
Email: study-info@unisa.ac.za
Phone: +27 (12) 429 3111
Fax: +27 (12) 429 3221
Year founded: 1873
Ownership: Nonprofit, state
Accreditation: Non-U.S. equivalent
Residency: None
Cost: $
Special fields: Educational management

Offers an M.Ed. in educational management. Students complete four to six intensive course modules and a thesis. All work can be completed by correspondence, though an increasing number of courses are also available online. No residency is required.

UNIVERSITY OF SOUTH ALABAMA

Office of Admissions
182 Administrative Building
Mobile, AL 36688-0002
Web site: usaonline.southalabama.edu
Email: admiss@usamail.usouthal.edu
Phone: (334) 460 6141 • (800) 872 5247
Fax: (334) 460 7876
Ownership: Nonprofit, state
Accreditation: Regional (Southern Association of Colleges and Schools)
Residency: None, generally
Cost: $$$
Special fields: Educational administration

Offers an M.Ed. with specialization in educational administration. The program is designed to meet Alabama state licensure requirements. All coursework can be completed online.

Adult and vocational education

Master's degree programs in this field prepare you to teach at an adult school (typically a division within the public school district) or in public or private vocational programs. Some of the emphasis options are Adult Basic Education (ABE), English as a Second Language (ESL), and vocational programs including automotive technology, plumbing, carpentry, nursing, and so on. A common use for such a master's degree is to become an administrator of these types of programs.

CAPELLA UNIVERSITY

222 South 9th Street, 20th Floor
Minneapolis, MN 55402-3389
Web site: www.capellauniversity.edu
Email: info@capella.edu
Phone: (612) 339 8650 • (888) 227 3552
Fax: (612) 337 5396
Year founded: 1993
Ownership: Proprietary
Accreditation: Regional (North Central Association of Colleges and Schools)
Residency: None
Cost: $$$$
Special fields: Adult education

Offers an M.S. in education with specialization in adult education. Students complete five core courses, four specialization courses, three elective courses, and a capstone project. All coursework may be completed online.

EDITH COWAN UNIVERSITY

International Students Office
Claremont, Western Australia 6010
Australia
Web site: www.cowan.edu.au
Email: extstudi@echidna.cowan.edu.au
Phone: +61 (9) 273 8681
Year founded: 1990
Ownership: Nonprofit
Accreditation: Non-U.S. equivalent
Residency: None
Cost: $$
Special fields: Career education

Offers an external M.Ed. in career education. Students may choose a coursework-only track (consisting of eight course modules), a coursework-and-project track (consisting of six course modules and a capstone project), or a capstone-and-thesis track (comprised of four course modules and a thesis). Students can complete the program in two to five years of part-time study. No residency is required.

INDIANA UNIVERSITY

Department of Adult Education
Union Building 507
Indianapolis, IN 46202
Web site: scs.indiana.edu
Email: adulted@iupui.edu
Phone: (317) 274 3472
Fax: (317) 278 2280
Year founded: 1912
Ownership: Nonprofit, state
Accreditation: Regional (North Central Association of Colleges and Schools)
Residency: None
Cost: $$$
Special fields: Adult education

The M.S. in adult education is available through a coursework-only track (requiring 12 courses) or a coursework-and-thesis track (requiring 10 courses and a thesis). Students are given six years to complete the program, which features a student-defined concentration of 9 to 12 semester hours. No residency is required.

NATIONAL-LOUIS UNIVERSITY

2480 Sheridan Road
Evanston, IL 60201
Web site: www.nl.edu

How did Susie ever get an "F" in P.E.?

Email: nluinfo@wheeling1.nl.edu
Phone: (847) 256 5156 • (800) 443 5522
Fax: (847) 256 1057
Year founded: 1886
Ownership: Nonprofit
Accreditation: Regional (North Central Association of Colleges and Schools)
Residency: None
Cost: $$$
Special fields: Adult education

The M.A. in adult education consists of five 8-week terms (each worth 6 semester hours of credit) and a presentation of a capstone inquiry, which is usually completed alongside the coursework rather than afterwards. No residency is required.

OPEN UNIVERSITY

Walton Hall
Milton Keynes MK7 6AA
United Kingdom
Web site: www.open.ac.uk
Email: ces-gen@open.ac.uk
Phone: +44 (190) 827 4066
Fax: +44 (190) 865 3744
Year founded: 1969
Ownership: Nonprofit
Accreditation: Non-U.S. equivalent
Residency: None
Cost: $$
Special fields: Lifelong learning management

The M.A. in education with emphasis in lifelong learning management consists of three extraordinarily intensive course modules. All coursework can be completed by correspondence, and no thesis is required.

PENNSYLVANIA STATE UNIVERSITY

207 Mitchell Building
University Park, PA 16802-3601
Web site: www.outreach.psu.edu/DE
Email: psude@cde.psu.edu
Phone: (814) 865 5403 • (800) 252 3592
Fax: (814) 865 3290
Year founded: 1855
Ownership: Nonprofit, state
Accreditation: Regional (Middle States Association of Colleges and Schools)
Residency: None
Cost: $$$
Special fields: Adult education

The M.Ed. in adult education consists of 11 classes that include both online and correspondence-based components. With faculty approval, students choose specific coursework to meet their individual needs. No thesis is required.

UNIVERSITY OF PRETORIA

Pretoria 0002
South Africa
Web site: www.up.ac.za/telematic
Email: telehelp@postino.up.ac.za
Phone: +27 (12) 420 3884
Fax: +27 (12) 362 5168
Year founded: 1930
Ownership: Nonprofit
Accreditation: Non-U.S. equivalent
Residency: Variable
Cost: $$
Special fields: Potential development in education & training

Offers an M.Ed. in potential development in education and training, based on a mix of correspondence, Web-based, and on-campus study.

Curriculum, instruction, and assessment

A master's degree in curriculum, instruction, and assessment (or one of its many variants) prepares teachers to be subject matter experts both on the school site and at the district level. If you have an interest in which things are taught, how things are taught, and how to "test" what has been taught, this could be the master's degree for you.

CAPELLA UNIVERSITY
222 South 9th Street, 20th Floor
Minneapolis, MN 55402-3389
Web site: www.capellauniversity.edu
Email: info@capella.edu
Phone: (612) 339 8650 • (888) 227 3552
Fax: (612) 337 5396
Year founded: 1993
Ownership: Proprietary
Accreditation: Regional (North Central Association of Colleges and Schools)
Residency: None
Cost: $$$$
Special fields: Teaching & learning

Offers an M.S. in education with emphasis in teaching and learning. Students complete 12 courses and a capstone project. All coursework may be completed online.

CITY UNIVERSITY
335 116th Avenue, SE
Bellevue, WA 98004
Web site: www.cityu.edu
Email: info@cityu.edu
Phone: (425) 637 1010 • (800) 426 5596
Fax: (425) 277 2437
Year founded: 1973
Ownership: Nonprofit, independent
Accreditation: Regional (Northwest Association of Schools and Colleges)
Residency: None
Cost: $$$$
Special fields: Curriculum & instruction

Offers an M.Ed. in curriculum and instruction consisting of 12 courses and the student's choice of a thesis, project, or internship. All coursework can be completed online, and no residency is required.

DEAKIN UNIVERSITY
Deakin International
336 Glenferrie Road
Malvern, Victoria 3144
Australia
Web site: www.deakin.edu.au
Phone: +61 (3) 9244 5095
Fax: +61 (3) 9244 5094
Year founded: 1974
Ownership: Nonprofit

Accreditation: Non-U.S. equivalent
Residency: None
Cost: $$
Special fields: Curriculum & administration studies

Offers an M.Ed. in curriculum and administration studies. Students may choose a coursework-only track or a coursework-and-research track. The program takes two to three years to complete via part-time study.

EDITH COWAN UNIVERSITY
International Students Office
Claremont, Western Australia 6010
Australia
Web site: www.cowan.edu.au
Email: extstudi@echidna.cowan.edu.au
Phone: +61 (9) 273 8681
Year founded: 1990
Ownership: Nonprofit
Accreditation: Non-U.S. equivalent
Residency: None
Cost: $$
Special fields: Teaching & learning

Offers an M.Ed. in teaching and learning. Students may choose a coursework-only track (comprised of eight course modules), a coursework-and-project track (comprised of six course modules and a capstone project), or a coursework-and-thesis track (comprised of four course modules and a thesis). Takes two to five years to complete. No residency is required.

GRAND CANYON UNIVERSITY
3300 West Camelback Road
Phoenix, AZ 85017
Web site: www.grand-canyon.edu
Email: admiss@grand-canyon.edu
Phone: (602) 589 2744 • (800) 600 5019
Year founded: 1949
Ownership: Nonprofit, independent
Accreditation: Regional (North Central Association of Colleges and Schools)
Residency: None
Cost: $$$$
Special fields: Teaching

Offers a Master of Arts in Teaching (M.A.T.) for working educators entirely through online study. Students must complete ten courses and a capstone project.

LAKEHEAD UNIVERSITY
Graduate Studies in Education
Faculty of Education
955 Oliver Road
Thunder Bay, ON P7B 5E1
Canada

Web site: www.lakeheadu.ca
Phone: +1 (807) 343 8054
Fax: +1 (807) 346 7771
Ownership: Nonprofit
Accreditation: Non-U.S. equivalent
Residency: None
Cost: $$$
Special fields: Curriculum studies

Offers an M.Ed. in curriculum studies by correspondence; an increasing number of courses are also available online. Students may choose a coursework-and-thesis track (consisting of two compulsory courses, three electives, a graduate seminar, and a thesis) or a coursework-and-project track (consisting of two compulsory courses, five electives, a graduate seminar, and a project).

REGENT UNIVERSITY

Graduate Center
1650 Diagonal Road
Alexandria, VA 22314-2857
Web site: www.regent.edu
Email: admissions@regent.edu
Phone: (757) 226 4127 • (800) 373 5504
Fax: (703) 740 1471
Year founded: 1977
Ownership: Nonprofit, independent
Accreditation: Regional (Southern Association of Colleges and Schools)
Residency: None
Cost: $$$$
Special fields: Master educator program

Offers an M.Ed. Master Educator program entirely through online study. Students complete ten courses and a capstone project. No residency is required.

UNIVERSITY OF ILLINOIS AT URBANA-CHAMPAIGN

Urbana, IL 61801
Web site: cter.ed.uiuc.edu
Email: graduate@admissions.uiuc.edu
Phone: (217) 333 1000
Fax: (217) 333 9758
Year founded: 1867
Ownership: Nonprofit, state
Accreditation: Regional (North Central Association of Colleges and Schools)
Residency: None
Cost: $$$
Special fields: Curriculum, technology, & education reform

The online M.Ed. in curriculum, technology, and education reform involves five core courses, five elective

courses, and a capstone project. Students can complete the program in about three years.

UNIVERSITY OF MARYLAND

University College
3501 University Boulevard, East
Adelphi, MD 20783
Web site: www.umuc.edu
Email: umucinfo@umuc.edu
Phone: (301) 985 7000 • (800) 888 8682
Fax: (301) 454 0399
Year founded: 1856
Ownership: Nonprofit, state
Accreditation: Regional (Middle States Association of Colleges and Schools)
Residency: Capstone seminar
Cost: $$$
Special fields: Teaching

The Master of Arts in Teaching (M.A.T.) meets Maryland state licensure requirements for basic teacher certification. The curriculum consists of nine courses and a capstone internship with seminar.

UNIVERSITY OF PHOENIX

4615 East Elwood Street
Phoenix, AZ 85072
Web site: www.phoenix.edu
Phone: (480) 966 9577 • (800) 742 4742
Fax: (480) 829 9030
Year founded: 1976
Ownership: Proprietary
Accreditation: Regional (North Central Association of Colleges and Schools)
Residency: None
Cost: $$$$
Special fields: Curriculum & instruction

Offers an online M.A. in education with emphasis in curriculum and instruction. Students must complete ten online courses and a capstone applied research project.

UNIVERSITY OF SOUTH ALABAMA

Office of Admissions
182 Administrative Building
Mobile, AL 36688-0002
Web site: usaonline.southalabama.edu
Email: admiss@usamail.usouthal.edu
Phone: (334) 460 6141 • (800) 872 5247
Fax: (334) 460 7876
Ownership: Nonprofit, state
Accreditation: Regional (Southern Association of Colleges and Schools)
Residency: None, generally

Cost: $$$
Special fields: Collaborative teacher education, instructional design & development

Offers an M.Ed. with specialization in collaborative teacher education, designed to meet Alabama's Class A teaching certification requirements. Also offers an M.S. in instructional design and development. All coursework can be completed online, but students seeking Class A certification may be required to attend some short residency sessions.

UNIVERSITY OF TEXAS

Office of Information Technology and
    Distance Education
201 West Seventh Street
Austin, TX 78701
Web site: www.telecampus.utsystem.edu
Email: telecampus@utsystem.edu
Phone: (512) 499 4207 • (888) 786 9832
Year founded: 1973
Ownership: Nonprofit, state
Accreditation: Regional (Southern Association
    of Colleges and Schools)
Residency: None
Cost: $$
Special fields: Curriculum & instruction (reading)

Offers an M.Ed. in curriculum and instruction with emphasis in reading. No thesis is required. This program prepares students to apply for the following certifications in Texas (assuming satisfactory grades on the relevant ExCET tests): Reading Specialist Certification, the Master Reading Teacher Certification, and English as a Second Language (ESL) Endorsement.

WALDEN UNIVERSITY

155 Fifth Avenue, South
Minneapolis, MN 55401
Web site: www.waldenu.edu
Email: info@waldenu.edu
Phone: (612) 338 7224 • (800) 925 3368
Fax: (612) 338 5092
Year founded: 1970
Ownership: Nonprofit, independent
Accreditation: Regional (North Central
    Association of Colleges and Schools)
Residency: Seminars
Cost: $$$$
Special fields: Classroom education, educational
    change & innovation

Offers an M.S. in education with specialization in classroom education or educational change and innovation. This program can be completed in as little as 18 months. Students must attend seminars on a semi-regular basis; these are held at a variety of locations nationwide. The program consists of ten courses and a capstone residential seminar.

Distance education

Like everything else in education, real competence in distance teaching takes a certain knowledge base. A master's degree in distance education prepares you either to teach via distance learning or, more likely, to work on the design and administration of a distance education program. Distance education programs are not only at the university level; many public school districts are now exploring the applications possible with this "new" medium.

ATHABASCA UNIVERSITY

1 University Drive
Athabasca, AB T9S 3A3
Canada
Web site: cde.athabascau.ca
Email: mde@athabascau.ca
Phone: (780) 675 6100 • (800) 788 9041
Fax: (780) 675 6145
Year founded: 1970
Ownership: Nonprofit
Accreditation: Non-U.S. equivalent
Residency: None
Cost: $$$
Special fields: Distance education

The online Master of Distance Education (MDE) is a professional program offered through Athabasca University's well-known Centre for Distance Education. Students may choose one of two routes: the thesis/project route (which involves three course modules and a capstone thesis or project) or the course-based route (which involves seven course modules and a final examination). No residency is required.

CALIFORNIA STATE UNIVERSITY—HAYWARD

Extended and Continuing Education
25800 Carlos Bee Boulevard
Hayward, CA 94542-3012
Web site: www.online.csuhayward.edu
Email: online@csuhayward.edu
Phone: (510) 885 3605
Fax: (510) 885 4817
Year founded: 1957
Ownership: Nonprofit, state
Accreditation: Regional (Western Association
    of Schools and Colleges)

Residency: None

Cost: $$

Special fields: Online teaching & learning

Offers an M.S. in education with a concentration in online teaching and learning. No residency is required. The program consists of nine courses (all of them focusing on online instruction) and a final thesis or project.

CAPELLA UNIVERSITY

222 South 9th Street, 20th Floor

Minneapolis, MN 55402-3389

Web site: www.capellauniversity.edu

Email: info@capella.edu

Phone: (612) 339 8650 • (888) 227 3552

Fax: (612) 337 5396

Year founded: 1993

Ownership: Proprietary

Accreditation: Regional (North Central Association of Colleges and Schools)

Residency: None

Cost: $$$$

Special fields: Distance education, instructional design for online learning, teaching & training online

Offers an M.S. in education with specialization in distance education, instructional design for online learning, or teaching and training online. Students complete 12 courses and a capstone project. All work may be completed online.

"But I honestly had no idea Linda Ronstadt was a silicon crystal!"

CURTIN UNIVERSITY OF TECHNOLOGY

G.P.O. Box U 1987

Perth, Western Australia 6845

Australia

Web site: www.curtin.edu.au

Email: customer-service@curtin.edu.au

Fax: +61 (8) 9266 9266

Year founded: 1967

Ownership: Nonprofit

Accreditation: Non-U.S. equivalent

Residency: None

Cost: $$

Special fields: Internet studies (education & training)

The Master of Internet Studies in education and training involves five core modules and a final project. All coursework can be completed online.

JONES INTERNATIONAL UNIVERSITY

9697 East Mineral Avenue

Englewood, CO 80112

Web site: www.international.edu

Email: info@international.edu

Phone: (303) 784 8045 • (800) 811 5663

Fax: (303) 784 8547

Year founded: 1995

Ownership: Proprietary

Accreditation: Regional (North Central Association of Colleges and Schools)

Residency: None

Cost: $$$

Special fields: e-Learning

Offers an online M.Ed. in e-Learning with optional specialization tracks in corporate training and knowledge management, global leadership and administration, library and resource management, research and assessment, or technology and design. Students take five core courses, two elective courses, four specialization courses, a production module, and a capstone project. Up to nine hours of credit (three courses worth) may be awarded on the basis of transfer credit, prior work experience, or other documented learning.

MARLBORO COLLEGE

Graduate Center

28 Vernon Street, Suite 5

Brattleboro, VT 05301

Web site: www.gradcenter.marlboro.edu

Email: gradcenter@marlboro.edu

Phone: (802) 258 9200 • (888) 258 5665

Fax: (802) 258 9201

Year founded: 1946

Ownership: Nonprofit, independent

Accreditation: Regional (New England Association of Schools and Colleges)

Residency: Two Friday night/Saturday morning residencies per month

Cost: $$$$

Special fields: Teaching with Internet technologies

Offers a low-residency Master of Arts in Teaching (M.A.T.) in teaching with Internet technologies. The program consists of eight online courses (supplemented by biweekly residencies, as described above), a capstone project, and a capstone seminar.

NOVA SOUTHEASTERN UNIVERSITY

3301 College Avenue
Fort Lauderdale, FL 33314

Web site: www.nova.edu

Email: cwis@nova.edu

Phone: (954) 262 8500 • (800) 541 6682

Year founded: 1964

Ownership: Nonprofit, independent

Accreditation: Regional (Southern Association of Colleges and Schools)

Residency: One extended weekend per semester and annual eight-day summer residencies

Cost: $$$$

Special fields: Instructional technology & distance education

Offers an M.S. in instructional technology and distance education. Students must attend three to six days of extended weekend sessions each semester (held in February–March and October–November) and an eight-day summer institute (held in July or August). Students progress through the program as part of a cohort of 20–25 students. The curriculum consists of eight study areas, each including individual assignments and a capstone team project. At the end of the program, each student must complete an individual practicum (applied capstone project).

OPEN UNIVERSITY

Walton Hall
Milton Keynes MK7 6AA
United Kingdom

Web site: www.open.ac.uk

Email: ces-gen@open.ac.uk

Phone: +44 (190) 827 4066

Fax: +44 (190) 865 3744

Year founded: 1969

Ownership: Nonprofit

Accreditation: Non-U.S. equivalent

Residency: None

Cost: $$

Special fields: Open & distance education

The M.A. in open and distance education consists of three intensive course modules (in distance learning information technology, open and distance learning implementation, and distributed/flexible learning). All coursework can be completed by correspondence, and no thesis is required.

ROYAL ROADS UNIVERSITY

2005 Sooke Road
Victoria, BC V9B 5Y2
Canada

Web site: www.royalroads.ca

Email: rrudistributedlearning@royalroads.ca

Phone: +1 (250) 391 2685 • (800) 788 8028

Fax: +1 (250) 391 2608

Year founded: 1995

Ownership: Nonprofit, state

Accreditation: Non-U.S. equivalent

Residency: Three-week residency

Cost: $$$

Special fields: Distributed learning

With the exception of the mandatory three-week residency (generally offered in August), the entire M.A. program in distributed learning may be completed online. Students complete four intensive course modules and a capstone project. It generally takes two years to complete the program.

UNIVERSITY OF LONDON

The External Programme
Senate House, Malet Street
London WC1E 7HU
England

Web site: www.lon.ac.uk/external

Email: enquiries@external.lon.ac.uk

Phone: +44 (20) 7862 8360

Fax: +44 (20) 7862 8358

Year founded: 1836

Ownership: Nonprofit

Accreditation: Non-U.S. equivalent

Residency: None

Cost: $$

Special fields: Distance education

The world's oldest external program offers an M.A. in distance education via examination. Students study on their own, and are required to pass a series of six rigorous examinations (proctored at Sylvan Learning Centers worldwide, among other locations) and complete a capstone project.

UNIVERSITY OF MARYLAND

University College
3501 University Boulevard, East
Adelphi, MD 20783
Web site: www.umuc.edu
Email: umucinfo@umuc.edu
Phone: (301) 985 7000 • (800) 888 8682
Fax: (301) 454 0399
Year founded: 1856
Ownership: Nonprofit, state
Accreditation: Regional (Middle States
    Association of Colleges and Schools)
Residency: None
Cost: $$$
Special fields: Distance education

The Master of Distance Education (MDE) consists of seven core courses, four elective courses, and a capstone project. All coursework can be completed online, and no residency is required.

UNIVERSITY OF PHOENIX

4615 East Elwood Street
Phoenix, AZ 85072
Web site: www.phoenix.edu
Phone: (480) 966 9577 • (800) 742 4742
Fax: (480) 829 9030
Year founded: 1976
Ownership: Proprietary
Accreditation: Regional (North Central
    Association of Colleges and Schools)
Residency: None
Cost: $$$$
Special fields: e-education

Offers an online M.A. in education with emphasis in e-education. Students must complete ten online courses and a capstone applied research project. No on-campus residency is required.

UNIVERSITY OF SOUTHERN QUEENSLAND

International Office
Toowoomba, Queensland 4350
Australia
Web site: www.usqonline.com.au
Email: international@usq.edu.au
Phone: +61 (7) 4631 2362
Fax: +61 (7) 4636 2211
Year founded: 1967
Ownership: Nonprofit
Accreditation: Non-U.S. equivalent
Residency: None
Cost: $$
Special fields: Online education,
    open & distance learning

The M.Ed. is available in either of the above fields. The open and distance learning major addresses more traditional distance learning formats as well as online study, and can be completed online or via correspondence. The M.Ed. in online education is only available online. Students complete eight modules and a capstone research project.

Educational technology

A quite popular program these days, a master's in educational technology is useful not only to the educational software programmer or the public school computer guru, but also to the classroom teacher. The curriculum goes beyond how to use the one computer in the classroom and focuses on which are the best uses for computers in education and how they should best be used by teachers in instructing students.

BOISE STATE UNIVERSITY

IPT Department, ET-338
College of Engineering
1910 University Drive
Boise, ID 83725
Web site: coen.boisestate.edu/dep/ipt.htm
Email: bsuipt@micron.net
Phone: (208) 426 1312 • (800) 824 7017, ext 1312
Fax: (208) 426 1970
Year founded: 1932
Ownership: Nonprofit, state
Accreditation: Regional (North Central
    Association of Colleges and Schools)
Residency: None
Cost: $$$
Special fields: Instructional &
    performance technology

Offers an M.S. in instructional and performance technology with no required on-campus residency. Students must complete 12 online courses and a comprehensive examination. No thesis is required. Up to nine hours may be transferred into the program with faculty approval.

CITY UNIVERSITY

335 116th Avenue, SE
Bellevue, WA 98004
Web site: www.cityu.edu
Email: info@cityu.edu
Phone: (425) 637 1010 • (800) 426 5596
Fax: (425) 277 2437
Year founded: 1973

Ownership: Nonprofit, independent
Accreditation: Regional (Northwest Association of Schools and Colleges)
Residency: None
Cost: $$$$
Special fields: Educational technology

The online M.Ed. in educational technology consists of eight core courses in education, four specialization courses in educational technology, and a student's choice of a thesis, project, or internship. No residency is required.

EDITH COWAN UNIVERSITY

International Students Office
Claremont, Western Australia 6010
Australia
Web site: www.cowan.edu.au
Email: extstudi@echidna.cowan.edu.au
Phone: +61 (9) 273 8681
Year founded: 1990
Ownership: Nonprofit
Accreditation: Non-U.S. equivalent
Residency: None
Cost: $$
Special fields: Educational computing, interactive multimedia

Offers an M.Ed. in either of the fields listed above; students may choose a coursework-only track (comprised of eight course modules), a coursework-and-project track (comprised of six course modules and a capstone project), or a coursework-and-thesis track (comprised of four course modules and a thesis). Takes two to five years to complete. No residency is required.

EMPORIA STATE UNIVERSITY

1200 Commercial
Box 4052
Emporia, KS 66801-5087
Web site: lifelong.emporia.edu
Email: lifelong@emporia.edu
Phone: (316) 341 5385
Fax: (316) 341 5744
Year founded: 1863
Ownership: Nonprofit, state
Accreditation: Regional (North Central Association of Colleges and Schools)
Residency: None
Cost: $$$
Special fields: Instructional design & technology

The M.S. in instructional design and technology consists of nine core courses, three elective courses, and a capstone project. The program can be completed entirely through online study.

FLORIDA GULF COAST UNIVERSITY

Distance Learning Program
10501 FGCU Boulevard
Fort Myers, FL 33908-4500
Web site: www.fgcu.edu/DL
Email: tdugas@fgcu.edu
Phone: (941) 590 2315
Year founded: 1997
Ownership: Nonprofit
Accreditation: Regional (Southern Association of Colleges and Schools)
Residency: None
Cost: $$$
Special fields: Curriculum & instruction (educational technology)

FGCU's College of Education offers two online master's programs in educational technology: the M.Ed., for Florida certified teachers, and the M.A., for those who do not possess (or plan to seek) certification in Florida. The program requirements for the two programs appear identical, each requiring a total of 12 courses. All coursework may be completed online, and no residency is required.

GEORGE WASHINGTON UNIVERSITY

The Graduate School of Education and Human Development
Master's Degree Program, Educational Technology Leadership
2134 G Street, NW
Washington, DC 20052
Web site: www.gwu.edu/~etl
Email: etlinfo@gwu.edu
Phone: (202) 994 9295 • (866) 498 3382
Year founded: 1821
Ownership: Nonprofit
Accreditation: Regional (Middle States Association of Colleges and Schools)
Residency: None
Cost: $$$
Special fields: Educational technology leadership

Offers an M.A. in education and human development with specialization in educational technology leadership, entirely through online study. Students must complete nine core courses and three elective courses. No residency is required.

NOVA SOUTHEASTERN UNIVERSITY

3301 College Avenue
Fort Lauderdale, FL 33314
Web site: www.nova.edu
Email: cwis@nova.edu
Phone: (954) 262 8500 • (800) 541 6682

Year founded: 1964
Ownership: Nonprofit, independent
Accreditation: Regional (Southern Association of Colleges and Schools)
Residency: One extended weekend session per semester and annual eight-day summer residencies
Cost: $$$$
Special fields: Computing technology in education, instructional technology & distance education

Offers online M.S. programs in the above fields. Students must attend three to six days of extended weekend sessions each semester (held in February–March and October–November) and an eight-day summer institute (held in July or August). Students progress through the program as part of a cohort of 20–25 students. The curriculum consists of eight study areas, each including individual assignments and a capstone team project. At the end of the program, each student must complete an individual practicum (applied capstone project).

PEPPERDINE UNIVERSITY

24255 Pacific Coast Highway
Malibu, CA 90263
Web site: www.pepperdine.edu
Email: admission-seaver@pepperdine.edu
Phone: (310) 456 4000
Fax: (310) 456 4357
Year founded: 1937
Ownership: Nonprofit, independent
Accreditation: Regional (Western Association of Schools and Colleges)
Residency: Three face-to-face sessions
Cost: $$$$
Special fields: Educational technology

Offers an M.A. in educational technology entirely online except for three face-to-face sessions. The first two occur during an initial five-day intensive seminar at Pepperdine's West Los Angeles campus, and the other may take place at any of a number of approved national technology conference venues (the Florida Educational Technology Conference is cited as one example). Remaining requirements consist of 12 courses, which may be taken online.

UNIVERSITY OF ILLINOIS AT URBANA-CHAMPAIGN

Urbana, IL 61801
Web site: cter.ed.uiuc.edu
Email: graduate@admissions.uiuc.edu
Phone: (217) 333 1000
Fax: (217) 333 9758

Year founded: 1867
Ownership: Nonprofit, state
Accreditation: Regional (North Central Association of Colleges and Schools)
Residency: None
Cost: $$$

The online M.Ed. in curriculum, technology, and education reform involves five core courses, five elective courses, and a capstone project. Students can complete the program in about three years.

UNIVERSITY OF MANCHESTER

School of Education
Oxford Road
Manchester M13 9PL
United Kingdom
Web site: distlearn.man.ac.uk/dl
Email: distance.admin@man.ac.uk
Phone: +44 (16) 1275 3967
Year founded: 1851
Accreditation: Non-U.S. equivalent
Ownership: Nonprofit
Residency: Usually none
Cost: $$$
Special fields: Educational technology in English language teaching

The M.Ed., focusing on technology in English language teaching, involves six intensive course modules and a capstone thesis of 15,000–20,000 words. All requirements can be completed at a distance through a mix of online and correspondence coursework.

UNIVERSITY OF MARYLAND

University College
3501 University Boulevard, East
Adelphi, MD 20783
Web site: www.umuc.edu
Email: umucinfo@umuc.edu
Phone: (301) 985 7000 • (800) 888 8682
Fax: (301) 454 0399
Year founded: 1856
Ownership: Nonprofit, state
Accreditation: Regional (Middle States Association of Colleges and Schools)
Residency: None
Cost: $$$
Special fields: Instructional technology

The M.Ed. in instructional technology is made up of four core courses, four instructional technology courses, two special topics courses, and a capstone project. All coursework can be completed online; no residency is required.

UNIVERSITY OF MELBOURNE

Victoria, 3010
Australia
Web site: www.unimelb.edu.au/research
Email: j.gilbert@sgs.unimelb.edu.au
Phone: +61 (3) 8344 8670
Ownership: Nonprofit
Accreditation: Non-U.S. equivalent
Residency: Negotiable
Cost: $$
Special fields: Computer-assisted
    language learning

One of the most prestigious research universities in Australia, Melbourne makes its research M.Phil. programs available to students worldwide who are able to find, and work through, an approved local institution (the list of approved institutions is already fairly extensive, and students may petition to have new institutions added to the list). The program involves two to five years of study and a dissertation of about 60,000 words.

UNIVERSITY OF NORTHERN IOWA

1227 West 27th Street
Cedar Falls, IA 50614
Web site: www.uni.edu
Email: contined@uni.edu
Phone: (319) 273 2121 • (800) 772 1746
Year founded: 1847
Ownership: Nonprofit, state
Accreditation: Regional (North Central
    Association of Colleges and Schools)
Residency: Regional classroom meetings and
    on-campus summer intensives
Cost: $$$
Special fields: Educational technology

The M.A. in education with emphasis in educational technology can be completed through a mix of online study, regional extension workshops, and summer intensive seminars.

UNIVERSITY OF PHOENIX

4615 East Elwood Street
Phoenix, AZ 85072
Web site: www.phoenix.edu
Phone: (480) 966 9577 • (800) 742 4742
Fax: (480) 829 9030
Year founded: 1976
Ownership: Proprietary
Accreditation: Regional (North Central
    Association of Colleges and Schools)
Residency: None
Cost: $$$$

Special fields: Curriculum & technology

The online M.A. in education with emphasis in curriculum and technology consists of ten online courses and a capstone applied research project.

UNIVERSITY OF PRETORIA

Pretoria 0002
South Africa
Web site: www.up.ac.za/telematic
Email: telehelp@postino.up.ac.za
Phone: +27 (12) 420 3884
Fax: +27 (12) 362 5168
Year founded: 1930
Ownership: Nonprofit
Accreditation: Non-U.S. equivalent
Cost: $$
Residency: Variable
Special fields: Computer-assisted education

Offers an M.Ed. in computer-assisted education through a mix of correspondence, Web-based, and on-campus study.

UNIVERSITY OF SOUTH ALABAMA

Office of Admissions
182 Administrative Building
Mobile, AL 36688-0002
Web site: usaonline.southalabama.edu
Email: admiss@usamail.usouthal.edu
Phone: (334) 460 6141 • (800) 872 5247
Fax: (334) 460 7876
Ownership: Nonprofit, state
Accreditation: Regional (Southern Association
    of Colleges and Schools)
Residency: None
Cost: $$$
Special fields: Educational media

Offers an online M.Ed. in educational media. No thesis is required.

UNIVERSITY OF SOUTHERN QUEENSLAND

International Office
Toowoomba, Queensland 4350
Australia
Web site: www.usqonline.com.au
Email: international@usq.edu.au
Phone: +61 (7) 4631 2362
Fax: +61 (7) 4636 2211
Year founded: 1967
Ownership: Nonprofit
Accreditation: Non-U.S. equivalent
Residency: None
Cost: $$
Special fields: Educational technology

Offers an M.Ed. in educational technology, consisting of eight modules and a capstone research project. All coursework may be completed online.

UNIVERSITY OF TEXAS

Office of Information Technology and
 Distance Education
201 West Seventh Street
Austin, TX 78701
Web site: www.telecampus.utsystem.edu
Email: telecampus@utsystem.edu
Phone: (512) 499 4207 • (888) 786 9832
Year founded: 1973
Ownership: Nonprofit, state
Accreditation: Regional (Southern Association
 of Colleges and Schools)
Residency: None
Cost: $$
Special fields: Educational technology

The M.Ed. in educational technology is comprised of two core courses in curriculum and instruction, six in educational technology, and four electives. No thesis is required. All coursework can be completed online.

UNIVERSITY OF WYOMING

Department of Adult Learning and Technology
P.O. Box 3374, Education Building, Room 1
Laramie, WY 82071-3374
Web site: ecampus.uwyo.edu
Phone: (307) 766 3247
Year founded: 1886
Ownership: Nonprofit, state
Accreditation: Regional (North Central
 Association of Colleges and Schools)
Residency: One week
Cost: $$$
Special fields: Instructional technology

The M.S. in education specializing in instructional technology consists of ten online courses, a week-long residency (held at an extension site in Wyoming's scenic Snowy Range mountains), and a capstone project.

WALDEN UNIVERSITY

155 Fifth Avenue, South
Minneapolis, MN 55401
Web site: www.waldenu.edu
Email: info@waldenu.edu
Phone: (612) 338 7224 • (800) 925 3368
Fax: (612) 338 5092
Year founded: 1970
Ownership: Nonprofit, independent
Accreditation: Regional (North Central
 Association of Colleges and Schools)

Residency: Extension-site seminars
Cost: $$$$
Special fields: Educational technology

Offers an M.S. in education with specialization in educational technology. This program can be completed in as little as 18 months. Students must attend seminars on a semi-regular basis; these are held at a variety of locations nationwide. The program consists of ten courses and a capstone residential seminar.

K–12 and early childhood education

A master's degree in K–12 education prepares someone to become a public or private school teacher. An additional use for such a degree would be to fulfill a requirement for entering a doctoral program.

A master's degree in early childhood education focuses on those skills necessary to teach, or be an administrator for, the very young: preschool or kindergarten to third-grade levels.

CONCORDIA UNIVERSITY

275 Syndicate Street North
St. Paul, MN 55104
Web site: www.csp.edu/hspd
Email: cshs@csp.edu
Phone: (651) 641 8897 • (800) 211 3370
Fax: (651) 603 6144
Year founded: 1893
Ownership: Nonprofit, church
Accreditation: Regional (Middle States
 Association of Colleges and Schools)
Residency: One initial five-day residency
Cost: $$$
Special fields: Early childhood education

Offers an M.A. in education with emphasis in early childhood education. Students must attend an initial five-day residency, but all other work may be completed online. The program concludes with a capstone seminar (which must be a thesis, an appropriate portfolio, or another approved project).

EDITH COWAN UNIVERSITY

International Students Office
Claremont, Western Australia 6010
Australia
Web site: www.cowan.edu.au
Email: extstudi@echidna.cowan.edu.au
Phone: +61 (9) 273 8681

Year founded: 1990
Ownership: Nonprofit
Accreditation: Non-U.S. equivalent
Residency: None
Cost: $$
Special fields: Early childhood studies

Offers an external M.Ed. in early childhood studies. Students may choose a coursework-only track (comprised of eight course modules), a coursework-and-project track (comprised of six course modules and a capstone project), or a coursework-and-thesis track (comprised of four course modules and a thesis). Takes two to five years to complete. No residency is required.

LIBERTY UNIVERSITY

1971 University Boulevard
Lynchburg, VA 24502-2269
Web site: www.liberty.edu
Email: admissions@liberty.edu
Phone: (804) 582 2000 • (800) 424 9595
Fax: (804) 582 2304
Year founded: 1971
Ownership: Nonprofit, independent
Accreditation: Regional (Southern Association of Colleges and Schools)
Residency: Variable
Cost: $$$$
Special fields: Elementary education, secondary education

Offers a low-residency M.Ed. in the fields listed above; both programs are designed to meet Virginia state licensure requirements. Students are required to complete four core courses, four concentration courses, and four professional courses (five for students seeking Virginia state teaching licensure). No thesis is required. Students may be required to take coursework in residence; in particular, all students seeking Virginia state licensure must take at least nine hours of residential coursework (though this coursework is available in a special intensive format and can be completed during summer residencies).

NOVA SOUTHEASTERN UNIVERSITY

3301 College Avenue
Fort Lauderdale, FL 33314
Web site: www.nova.edu
Email: cwis@nova.edu
Phone: (954) 262 8500 • (800) 541 6682
Year founded: 1964
Ownership: Nonprofit, independent
Accreditation: Regional (Southern Association of Colleges and Schools)
Residency: One extended weekend session

per semester and annual eight-day summer residencies
Cost: $$$$
Special fields: Child & youth studies (early childhood education)

Offers an online M.S. program in child and youth studies with emphasis in early childhood education. Students must attend three to six days of extended weekend sessions each semester (held in February–March and October–November) and an eight-day summer institute (held in July or August). Students progress through the program as part of a cohort of 20–25 students; the curriculum consists of eight study areas, each including individual assignments and a capstone team project. At the end of the program, each student must complete an individual practicum (applied capstone project).

UNIVERSITY OF NORTHERN IOWA

1227 West 27th Street
Cedar Falls, IA 50614
Web site: www.uni.edu
Email: contined@uni.edu
Phone: (319) 273 2121 • (800) 772 1746
Year founded: 1847
Ownership: Nonprofit, state
Accreditation: Regional (North Central Association of Colleges and Schools)
Residency: Regional classroom meetings and on-campus summer intensives
Cost: $$$
Special fields: Elementary reading & language arts, middle school education, middle school mathematics

Offers the above programs through a combination of online study, regional extension workshops, and summer intensive seminars.

UNIVERSITY OF SOUTH AFRICA

P.O. Box 392
Unisa 0003
South Africa
Web site: www.unisa.ac.za
Email: study-info@unisa.ac.za
Phone: +27 (12) 429 3111
Fax: +27 (12) 429 3221
Year founded: 1873
Ownership: Nonprofit, state
Accreditation: Non-U.S. equivalent
Residency: None
Cost: $
Special fields: Gifted child education, preprimary education, primary education, secondary education

Well, there's no money for curriculum, but we have the best school cafeteria west of the Pecos!

Offers an M.Ed. in the above fields. Students complete four to six intensive course modules and a thesis. All work can be completed by correspondence, though an increasing number of courses are also available online.

Language and literacy education

Programs in the general areas of language and literacy education can prepare someone for a variety of teaching careers. These include teaching English as a second language both here and abroad, or being an early literacy specialist with students at the primary level (grades K–3), or, as is the case in many U.S. states with high rates of English language learners, just being a better classroom teacher for children who are refugees or recent immigrants.

ASTON UNIVERSITY
Language Studies Unit
Aston Triangle
Birmingham B4 7ET
United Kingdom
Web site: www.les.aston.ac.uk/lsu
Email: lsu@aston.ac.uk
Phone: +44 (12) 1359 3611
Fax: +44 (12) 1359 2725
Year founded: 1895

Ownership: Nonprofit
Accreditation: Non-U.S. equivalent
Residency: None
Cost: $$
Special fields: Teaching English

The M.S. in teaching English is a highly flexible program consisting of eight modules (courses) and a dissertation (thesis). The program can be tailored to the field of (TESOL), or to teaching English for other special purposes.

AZUSA PACIFIC UNIVERSITY
901 E. Alosta Avenue
P.O. Box 7000
Azusa, CA 91702-7000
Web site: www.apu.edu/tesol/field
Phone: (626) 815 3844 • (800) 366 3542
Year founded: 1965
Ownership: Nonprofit, independent
Accreditation: Regional (Western Association of Schools and Colleges)
Residency: Special (see below)
Cost: $$$
Special fields: Teaching English to speakers of other languages (TESOL)

Offers a special field-based M.A. in TESOL for students who wish to teach English in Asia while earning a degree. Students visit Azusa for intensive study sessions, complete assignments while abroad, and return for new assignments. The program can be completed in two and a half to three years.

CITY UNIVERSITY
335 116th Avenue, SE
Bellevue, WA 98004
Web site: www.cityu.edu
Email: info@cityu.edu
Phone: (425) 637 1010 • (800) 426 5596
Fax: (425) 277 2437
Year founded: 1973
Ownership: Nonprofit, independent
Accreditation: Regional (Northwest Association of Schools and Colleges)
Residency: None
Cost: $$$$
Special fields: Reading & literacy

The online M.Ed. in reading and literacy consists of eight core courses in education, four specialization courses in literacy education, and the student's choice of a thesis, project, or internship. No residency is required.

DEAKIN UNIVERSITY

Deakin International
336 Glenferrie Road
Malvern, Victoria 3144
Australia
Web site: www.deakin.edu.au
Phone: +61 (3) 9244 5095
Fax: +61 (3) 9244 5094
Year founded: 1974
Ownership: Nonprofit
Accreditation: Non-U.S. equivalent
Residency: None
Cost: $$
Special fields: Language & literacy education,
TESOL, teaching languages other than English

Offers a Master of Education in the fields listed above; students may choose a coursework-only track or a coursework-and-research track. The program takes two to three years to complete via part-time study.

EDITH COWAN UNIVERSITY

International Students Office
Claremont, Western Australia 6010
Australia
Web site: www.cowan.edu.au
Email: extstudi@echidna.cowan.edu.au
Phone: +61 (9) 273 8681
Year founded: 1990
Ownership: Nonprofit
Accreditation: Non-U.S. equivalent
Residency: None
Cost: $$
Special fields: Applied linguistics,
language & literacy

Offers an M.Ed. externally in either of the fields listed above; students may choose a coursework-only track (comprised of eight course modules), a coursework-and-project track (comprised of six course modules and a capstone project), or a coursework-and-thesis track (comprised of four course modules and a thesis). Takes two to five years to complete.

LIBERTY UNIVERSITY

1971 University Boulevard
Lynchburg, VA 24502-2269
Web site: www.liberty.edu
Email: admissions@liberty.edu
Phone: (804) 582 2000 • (800) 424 9595
Fax: (804) 582 2304
Year founded: 1971
Ownership: Nonprofit, independent
Accreditation: Regional (Southern Association
of Colleges and Schools)

Residency: Variable
Cost: $$$$
Special fields: Reading specialist

Offers a low-residency M.Ed. Reading Specialist program, designed to meet Virginia state licensure requirements. Students are required to complete four core courses, four concentration courses, and four professional courses (five for students seeking Virginia state teaching licensure). No thesis is required. Students may be required to take coursework in residence; in particular, all students seeking Virginia state licensure must take at least nine hours of residential coursework (though this coursework is available in a special intensive format and can be completed during summer residencies).

MONASH UNIVERSITY

Distance Education Centre
Gippsland Campus
Northways Road
Churchill, Victoria 3842
Australia
Web site: www.monash.edu.au/de
Email: course.inquiries@celts.monash.edu.au
Phone: +61 (3) 9902 6200
Fax: +61 (3) 9902 6300
Year founded: 1961
Ownership: Nonprofit
Accreditation: Non-U.S. equivalent
Residency: None
Cost: $$
Special fields: Applied linguistics

The M.A. in applied linguistics consists of eight core course modules; no thesis is required. Coursework takes place primarily via correspondence (supplemented in some cases with autocassettes); an increasing number of courses are also available online.

OPEN UNIVERSITY

Walton Hall
Milton Keynes MK7 6AA
United Kingdom
Web site: www.open.ac.uk
Email: ces-gen@open.ac.uk
Phone: +44 (190) 827 4066
Fax: +44 (190) 865 3744
Year founded: 1969
Ownership: Nonprofit
Accreditation: Non-U.S. equivalent
Residency: None
Cost: $$
Special fields: Applied linguistics

The M.A. in education with emphasis in applied

linguistics consists of three extraordinarily intensive course modules. All coursework can be completed by correspondence, and no thesis is required.

REGENT UNIVERSITY

Graduate Center
1650 Diagonal Road
Alexandria, VA 22314-2857
Web site: www.regent.edu
Email: admissions@regent.edu
Phone: (757) 226 4127 • (800) 373 5504
Fax: (703) 740 1471
Year founded: 1977
Ownership: Nonprofit, independent
Accreditation: Regional (Southern Association
    of Colleges and Schools)
Residency: Variable
Cost: $$$$
Special fields: Teaching English to students
    of other languages (TESOL)

Offers a low-residency master's in TESOL. Students are required to complete ten online courses and a capstone project.

UNIVERSITY OF KENT AT CANTERBURY

The Registry
Canterbury, Kent CT2 7NZ
United Kingdom
Web site: www.ukc.ac.uk
Email: graduate-office@ukc.ac.uk
Phone: +44 (12) 2782 4040
Fax: +44 (12) 2745 2196
Year founded: 1965
Ownership: Nonprofit
Accreditation: Non-U.S. equivalent
Residency: Negotiable
Cost: $$$
Special fields: Applied linguistics

Offers a research-based M.Phil. in applied linguistics. Students work through an approved local facility and visit Kent for yearly residencies of negotiable duration. The program takes two to five years to complete.

UNIVERSITY OF LEICESTER

University Road
Leicester LE1 7RH
United Kingdom
Web site: www.le.ac.uk
Email: higherdegrees@le.ac.uk
Phone: +44 (11) 6252 2298
Fax: +44 (11) 6252 2200
Year founded: 1921
Ownership: Nonprofit

Accreditation: Non-U.S. equivalent
Residency: None
Cost: $$$
Special fields: Applied linguistics & TESOL

The M.A. in applied linguistics and TESOL consists of four core modules, two elective modules, and a dissertation (thesis) of 20,000 words. All work may be completed by correspondence.

UNIVERSITY OF MANCHESTER

School of Education
Oxford Road
Manchester M13 9PL
United Kingdom
Web site: distlearn.man.ac.uk/dl
Email: distance.admin@man.ac.uk
Phone: +44 (16) 1275 3967
Year founded: 1851
Accreditation: Non-U.S. equivalent
Ownership: Nonprofit
Residency: Usually none
Cost: $$$
Special fields: English language teaching,
    educational technology in English
    language teaching

The M.Ed. programs in the above fields involve six intensive course modules and a capstone thesis of 15,000 to 20,000 words. All requirements can be completed at a distance through a mix of online and correspondence coursework.

UNIVERSITY OF MELBOURNE

Victoria, 3010
Australia
Web site: www.unimelb.edu.au/research
Email: j.gilbert@sgs.unimelb.edu.au
Phone: +61 (3) 8344 8670
Ownership: Nonprofit
Accreditation: Non-U.S. equivalent
Residency: Negotiable
Cost: $$
Special fields: Applied linguistics, computer-
    assisted language learning, English as a
    second language

One of the most prestigious research universities in Australia, Melbourne makes its research M.Phil. programs available to students worldwide who are able to find, and work through, an approved local institution (the list of approved institutions is already fairly extensive, and students may petition to have new institutions added to the list). The program involves two to five years of study and a dissertation of about 60,000 words.

UNIVERSITY OF NORTHERN IOWA

1227 West 27th Street
Cedar Falls, IA 50614
Web site: www.uni.edu
Email: contined@uni.edu
Phone: (319) 273 2121 • (800) 772 1746
Year founded: 1847
Ownership: Nonprofit, state
Accreditation: Regional (North Central
Association of Colleges and Schools)
Residency: Regional classroom meetings and
on-campus summer intensives
Cost: $$$
Special fields: Communication education, elemen-
tary reading & language arts

Offers the above programs through a combination of
online study, regional extension workshops, and sum-
mer intensive seminars.

UNIVERSITY OF TEXAS

Office of Information Technology and Distance
Education
201 West Seventh Street
Austin, TX 78701
Web site: www.telecampus.utsystem.edu
Email: telecampus@utsystem.edu
Phone: (512) 499 4207 • (888) 786 9832
Year founded: 1973
Ownership: Nonprofit, state
Accreditation: Regional (Southern Association
of Colleges and Schools)
Residency: None
Cost: $$
Special fields: Curriculum and instruction
(reading)

Offers an M.Ed. in curriculum and instruction with
emphasis in reading. No thesis is required. This
program prepares students to apply for the following
certifications in Texas (assuming satisfactory grades on
the relevant ExCET tests): Reading Specialist Certification, the Master Reading Teacher Certification, and
English as a Second Language (ESL) Endorsement.

Librarianship

Earning a master's in librarianship, depending on your state, will qualify you to be a public
school librarian. Warning: Some states will
require that you also (or instead) complete a
Library Media Teacher credential. As always,
check with your state's teacher licensing office.

CHARLES STURT UNIVERSITY

International Division
Locked Bag 676
Wagga Wagga, New South Wales 2678
Australia
Web site: www.csu.edu.au
Email: inquiry@csu.edu.au
Phone: +61 (2) 6933 2666
Fax: +61 (2) 6933 2799
Year founded: 1989
Ownership: Nonprofit
Accreditation: Non-U.S. equivalent
Residency: None
Cost: $$
Special fields: Library & information
management, teacher librarianship

The Master of Applied Science in library and informa-
tion management is recognized as a first-level profes-
sional award by ALIA (the Australian Library and
Information Association), and can be completed in
three years of part-time, off-campus study. An M.Ed. in
teacher librarianship is also available with a course-
work-only track (consisting of eight course modules)
and a coursework-with-project track (consisting of
six modules and a capstone project). It is possible to
complete either track in about two years of part-time
off-campus study.

CONNECTICUT STATE UNIVERSITY

501 Crescent Street
New Haven, CT 06515-1355
Web site: onlinecsu.ctstateu.edu
Email: mls@onlinecsu.ctstateu.edu
Phone: (203) 392 5781 • (888) 500 SCSU
Ownership: Nonprofit, state
Accreditation: Regional (New England Association
of Schools and Colleges) and Professional
(American Library Association)
Residency: None
Cost: $$$
Special fields: Library science

Offers a Master of Library Science (M.L.S.) entirely
through online study. This degree is also approved by
the Connecticut State Board of Education to grant
cross-endorsement to Connecticut certified teachers.
The program consists of 12 courses: 5 core courses and
7 electives. No residency is required.

CURTIN UNIVERSITY OF TECHNOLOGY

G.P.O. Box U 1987
Perth, Western Australia 6845
Australia

Web site: www.curtin.edu.au
Email: customer-service@curtin.edu.au
Fax: +61 (8) 9266 9266
Year founded: 1967
Ownership: Nonprofit
Accreditation: Non-U.S. equivalent
Residency: None
Cost: $$
Special fields: Information & library studies

The Master of Information Management, with tracks in information and library studies and records management and archives, can be completed online, by correspondence, or through a combination of the two.

DREXEL UNIVERSITY

College of Information Science and Technology
3141 Chestnut Street
Philadelphia, PA 19104-2875
Web site: www.cis.drexel.edu
Email: info@cis.drexel.edu
Phone: (215) 895 2474 • (800) 237 3935
Fax: (215) 895 1414
Year founded: 1891
Ownership: Nonprofit, independent
Accreditation: Regional (Middle States Association of Colleges and Schools) and Professional (American Library Association)
Residency: None
Cost: $$$$
Special fields: Library & information science (management of digital information)

The online M.S. in library and information science (with emphasis in management of digital information) consists of 12 core courses and 3 elective courses; no thesis or capstone project is required. Much of the program deals with information technology issues (distributed computing and networking, human-computer interaction, Internet information resource design, and such).

EMPORIA STATE UNIVERSITY

1200 Commercial
Box 4052
Emporia, KS 66801-5087
Web site: lifelong.emporia.edu
Email: lifelong@emporia.edu
Phone: (316) 341 5385
Fax: (316) 341 5744
Year founded: 1863
Ownership: Nonprofit, state
Accreditation: Regional (North Central Association of Colleges and Schools)
Residency: Variable

Cost: $$$
Special fields: Library science

Offers a Master of Library Science (M.L.S.) through a mix of online coursework and intensive on-campus courses taken in Topeka or Emporia, Kansas, depending on which courses are available online during a given term.

FLORIDA STATE UNIVERSITY

Tallahassee, FL 32306
Web site: www.fsu.edu/~distance
Email: students@oddl.fsu.edu
Phone: (850) 645 0393 • (877) 357 8283
Year founded: 1851
Ownership: Nonprofit, state
Accreditation: Regional (Southern Association of Colleges and Schools) and Professional (American Library Association)
Residency: None
Cost: $$$
Special fields: Information & library studies, open & distance learning

The M.S. in information and library studies (offered through the ALA-accredited School of Information Studies) involves 42 semester hours of coursework (14 courses). No thesis is required, and the entire program can be completed online. An M.A. in open and distance learning, designed in consultation with the Open University (U.K.), is also available through online study.

SYRACUSE UNIVERSITY

Independent Study Degree Programs
700 University Avenue
Syracuse, NY 13244-2530
Web site: www.yesu.syr.edu
Email: suisdp@uc.syr.edu
Phone: (315) 443 3480 • (800) 442 0501
Fax: (315) 443 4174
Year founded: 1870
Ownership: Nonprofit
Accreditation: Regional (Middle States Association of Colleges and Schools) and Professional (American Library Association)
Residency: Variable
Cost: $$$$
Special fields: Library science

According to the school's Web site, the Syracuse Master of Library Science (M.L.S.) is ranked third in the country by *U.S. News and World Report*. Students attend an introductory summer residency, then progress through the program taking a mix of Internet-only courses (where no residency is required) and Internet-and-

Planned cover illustration for the ill-fated Bears' Guide to the Best Mountaineering Degrees by Distance Learning.

seminar courses (where students attend a two- to four-day initial seminar and complete remaining course requirements online). The program consists of a seven-course core (two courses in general library science, three in information resources, and three in management and policy) and a concentration in information organization/retrieval/accessibility, information services and resources, or information systems design and management. Students may conclude the program with a capstone research project, applied project, or internship.

UNIVERSITY OF ARIZONA
Tucson, AZ 85721
Web site: www.eu.arizona.edu/dist
Email: distance@u.arizona.edu
Phone: (520) 621 8632 • (800) 478 9508
Fax: (520) 621 3269
Year founded: 1885
Ownership: Nonprofit, state
Accreditation: Regional (North Central Association of Colleges and Schools) and Professional (American Library Association)
Residency: 12 semester hours (1/3 of the program)
Cost: $$$
Special fields: Information resources & library science
Offers an M.A. in information resources and library

science where two-thirds of the program can be completed online. Residential requirements can be fulfilled during summer and winter intensives. Students have up to six years to complete the program.

UNIVERSITY OF NORTHERN IOWA
1227 West 27th Street
Cedar Falls, IA 50614
Web site: www.uni.edu
Email: contined@uni.edu
Phone: (319) 273 2121 • (800) 772 1746
Year founded: 1847
Ownership: Nonprofit, state
Accreditation: Regional (North Central Association of Colleges and Schools)
Residency: Regional classroom meetings and on-campus summer intensives
Cost: $$$
Special fields: Library science
Offers a Master of Library Science through a combination of online study, regional extension workshops, and summer intensive seminars.

UNIVERSITY OF WISCONSIN—MILWAUKEE
School of Library and Information Science
P.O. Box 413
Milwaukee, WI 53211
Web site: www.slis.uwm.edu
Email: info@slis.uwm.edu
Phone: (414) 229 4707 • (888) 349 3432
Fax: (414) 229 4848
Year founded: 1885
Ownership: Nonprofit, state
Accreditation: Regional (North Central Association of Colleges and Schools) and Professional (American Library Association)
Residency: None
Cost: $$$
Special fields: Library & information science
Ranked one of the top 20 library and information schools in the country by *U.S. News and World Report*, UWM's ALA-accredited School of Library and Information Science offers a Master of Library and Information Science entirely through online study with no required on-campus residency. The program consists of 36 semester hours (12 courses); up to 6 semester hours may be transferred from another program.

Religious education

CONCORDIA UNIVERSITY
275 Syndicate Street North
St. Paul, MN 55104

Web site: www.csp.edu/hspd
Email: cshs@csp.edu
Phone: (651) 641 8897 • (800) 211 3370
Fax: (651) 603 6144
Year founded: 1893
Ownership: Nonprofit, church
Accreditation: Regional (Middle States Association of Colleges and Schools)
Residency: One initial five-day residency
Cost: $$$
Special fields: Parish education & administration

Offers a low-residency M.A. program in parish education and administration. Students must attend an initial five-day residency, but all other work may be completed online. The program concludes with a capstone seminar (which must be a thesis, an appropriate portfolio, or another approved project).

EDITH COWAN UNIVERSITY

International Students Office
Claremont, Western Austalia 6010
Australia
Web site: www.cowan.edu.au
Email: extstudi@echidna.cowan.edu.au
Phone: +61 (9) 273 8681
Year founded: 1990
Ownership: Nonprofit
Accreditation: Non-U.S. equivalent
Residency: None
Cost: $$
Special fields: Religious education

Offers an M.Ed. in religious education by correspondence. Students may choose a coursework-only track (comprised of eight course modules), a coursework-and-project track (comprised of six course modules and a capstone project), or a coursework-and-thesis track (comprised of four course modules and a thesis). Takes two to five years to complete.

GLOBAL UNIVERSITY OF THE ASSEMBLIES OF GOD

1211 S. Glenstone Avenue
Springfield, MO 65804
Web site: www.globaluniversity.edu
Email: sgs@globaluniversity.edu
Phone: (800) 443 1083
Fax: (417) 862 0863
Year founded: 2000
Ownership: Nonprofit, church
Accreditation: DETC (Distance Education and Training Council)
Residency: None
Cost: $$$
Special fields: Ministerial studies (education)

The M.A. in ministerial studies with emphasis in education is available with a coursework-only track (consisting of four core courses in research and biblical hermeneutics, four courses in general education methods, and four courses in religious education) and a coursework-and-thesis track (consisting of the four core courses, three courses in general education methods, two courses in religious education, and a thesis). Coursework can be completed online or by correspondence. No residency is required.

MARYVALE INSTITUTE

Maryvale House, Old Oscott Hill
Kingstanding
Birmingham B44 9AG
United Kingdom
Web site: www.maryvale.ac.uk
Phone: +44 (121) 360 8118
Ownership: Nonprofit, church
Accreditation: Non-U.S. equivalent
Residency: Negotiable
Cost: $$$
Special fields: Roman Catholic religious education

Offers a research-based M.Phil. in Catholic studies with emphasis in religious education, in association with the Pontifical University in Ireland. Residency is negotiated on a case-by-case basis.

NAROPA UNIVERSITY

2130 Arapahoe Avenue
Boulder, CO 80302
Web site: www.naropa.edu
Email: admissions@naropa.edu
Phone: (303) 444 0202
Fax: (303) 444 0410
Ownership: Nonprofit, independent
Accreditation: Regional (North Central Association of Colleges and Schools)
Residency: Two summer sessions (46 days total)
Cost: $$$$
Special fields: Contemplative education

The M.A. in contemplative education is a low-residency program that draws from Naropa University's unique interfaith (predominantly Buddhist) heritage. Students attend two summer residencies, each of 23 days duration, and complete remaining coursework during the spring and fall semesters. A good many of the courses may be individualized; others address subjects such as sacred learning and spiritual development. A thesis is required. The program concludes with a four-day graduation ceremony, but students have the option of participating in the ceremony online.

REGENT UNIVERSITY

Graduate Center
1650 Diagonal Road
Alexandria, VA 22314-2857
Web site: www.regent.edu
Email: admissions@regent.edu
Phone: (757) 226 4127 • (800) 373 5504
Fax: (703) 740 1471
Year founded: 1977
Ownership: Nonprofit, independent
Accreditation: Regional (Southern Association
    of Colleges and Schools)
Residency: None
Cost: $$$$
Special fields: Christian school program

Regent University offers a wholly online M.Ed. Christian school program. Students are required to complete ten online courses and a capstone project.

SPERTUS COLLEGE

618 S. Michigan Avenue
Chicago, IL 60605
Web site: www.spertus.edu
Email: sijs@spertus.edu
Phone: (312) 322 9012 • (888) 322 1769
Fax: (312) 922 6406
Year founded: 1924
Ownership: Nonprofit, independent
Accreditation: Regional (North Central
    Association of Colleges and Schools)
Residency: None
Cost: $$$$
Special fields: Jewish education

The M.S. in Jewish education is designed specifically for religious educators. Students complete six core courses in Jewish studies, six courses in Jewish education, and three elective courses. No residency is required. Students must be able to read Hebrew mechanically (e.g., verbalize the Hebrew alphabet and recognize common Hebrew words); for students who have no background in Hebrew, or need a refresher class, a special correspondence course is available. Spertus College is an interdenominational Jewish institution and welcomes students of all religious backgrounds.

UNIVERSITY OF GLASGOW

22 Western Court
Glasgow G12 8SQ
United Kingdom
Web site: www.gla.ac.uk/Inter/GUIDE
Email: guide@mis.gla.ac.uk
Phone: +44 (14) 1330 3870

Fax: +44 (14) 1330 4079
Year founded: 1451
Ownership: Nonprofit
Accreditation: Non-U.S. equivalent
Residency: None
Cost: $$$
Special fields: Religious education

The Master of Religious Education (M.R.E.) is a broad, flexible program that can accommodate Christian-oriented and interfaith tracks equally well. Students choose 6 of a possible 12 modules (addressing such topics as religious ethics, liturgical studies, Christology, the historical Jesus, women in religion, and Buddhism). No thesis is required.

Single-subject teaching areas (except for language and religion, both listed separately)

Single-subject teaching refers to that teaching done at the secondary (junior or senior high school) level. This level, as opposed to elementary school teaching, requires that the teacher specialize in a specific area such as history or math.

CURTIN UNIVERSITY OF TECHNOLOGY

G.P.O. Box U 1987
Perth, Western Australia 6845
Australia
Web site: www.curtin.edu.au
Email: customer-service@curtin.edu.au
Fax: +61 (8) 9266 9266
Year founded: 1967
Ownership: Nonprofit
Accreditation: Non-U.S. equivalent
Residency: None
Cost: $$
Special fields: Science education

The M.S. in science education is available with a coursework track (requiring five core courses and three elective courses) and a research track (requiring three core courses, an elective course, and a thesis). Coursework can be completed online, by correspondence, or at times through a combination of the two.

DEAKIN UNIVERSITY

Deakin International
336 Glenferrie Road
Malvern, Victoria 3144
Australia
Web site: www.deakin.edu.au
Phone: +61 (3) 9244 5095

Fax: +61 (3) 9244 5094
Year founded: 1974
Ownership: Nonprofit
Accreditation: Non-U.S. equivalent
Residency: None
Cost: $$
Special fields: Arts & social education, information technology education, mathematics education, physical & health education, science & environmental education

Offers a Master of Education in the fields listed above. Students may choose a coursework-only track or a coursework-and-research track. The program takes two to three years to complete via part-time study.

DUQUESNE UNIVERSITY

600 Forbes Avenue
Pittsburgh, PA 15282
Web site: www2.duq.edu/distancelearning
Phone: (412) 396 5983
Fax: (412) 396 5479
Year founded: 1878
Ownership: Nonprofit, independent
Accreditation: Regional (Middle States Association of Colleges and Schools)
Residency: Summer sessions
Cost: $$$$
Special fields: Music education

The M.Mus. in music education is, so far as we know, the only program of its kind in North America. The program involves 20 semester hours of core coursework (dealing with music education, music history, and music theory) and 10 hours of elective coursework. Sixteen of the 30 total hours may be completed by distance learning; the remaining 14 hours are organized around summer residencies. In lieu of a thesis, students are expected to design a music portfolio as they progress through the program, which takes three to five years to complete.

EDITH COWAN UNIVERSITY

International Students Office
Claremont, Western Australia 6010
Australia
Web site: www.cowan.edu.au
Email: extstudi@echidna.cowan.edu.au
Phone: +61 (9) 273 8681
Year founded: 1990
Ownership: Nonprofit
Accreditation: Non-U.S. equivalent
Residency: None
Cost: $$
Special fields: Mathematics education, music

education, science education, society & environment education, technology & enterprise education, visual arts education

Offers an M.Ed. externally in the fields listed above. Students may choose a coursework-only track (comprised of eight course modules), a coursework-and-project track (comprised of six course modules and a capstone project), or a coursework-and-thesis track (comprised of four course modules and a thesis). Takes two to five years to complete. No residency is required.

EMPORIA STATE UNIVERSITY

1200 Commercial
Box 4052
Emporia, KS 66801-5087
Web site: lifelong.emporia.edu
Email: lifelong@emporia.edu
Phone: (316) 341 5385
Fax: (316) 341 5744
Year founded: 1863
Ownership: Nonprofit, state
Accreditation: Regional (North Central Association of Colleges and Schools)
Residency: None
Cost: $$$
Special fields: Business education, physical education

The Master of Business Education (M.B.E.) consists of 35 semester hours of coursework. No thesis is required, but students must complete a capstone project. The program can be completed in about three years. The M.S. in physical education is available with a thesis track (consisting of 10 courses and a thesis) or a project track (consisting of 12 courses and a capstone project). Either program can be completed entirely online with no on-campus residency involved.

LESLEY UNIVERSITY

29 Everett Street
Cambridge, MA 02138-2790
Web site: www.lesley.edu
Email: info@mail.lesley.edu
Phone: (617) 349 8320 • (800) 999 1959
Fax: (617) 349 8313
Year founded: 1909
Ownership: Nonprofit, independent
Accreditation: Regional (New England Association of Schools and Colleges)
Residency: None
Cost: $$$
Special fields: Science in education, technology in education

The M.Ed. in science in education consists of six modules: one introductory module, and five interdisciplinary modules emphasizing direct education-related applications of scientific fields. The M.Ed. in technology in education consists of eight required courses and three elective courses for a total 33 semester hours of credit. Neither program requires a thesis or formal capstone project, and either program can be completed in about two years.

MONTANA STATE UNIVERSITY—BOZEMAN

Bozeman, MT 59717-2000
Web site: www.montana.edu
Email: gradstudy@montana.edu
Phone: (406) 994 4145
Year founded: 1893
Ownership: Nonprofit, state
Accreditation: Regional (Northwest
    Association of Schools and Colleges)
Residency: Negotiable
Cost: $$$
Special fields: Mathematics education,
    science education

Offers an M.S. in mathematics with emphasis in mathematics education; students design an individualized program in cooperation with faculty. Most of the program can be completed at a distance, though residency at some summer intensive seminars may be required. An M.S. in science education is also available.

PRESCOTT COLLEGE

220 Grove Avenue
Prescott, AZ 86301
Web site: www.prescott.edu
Email: admissions@prescott.edu
Phone: (520) 778 2090 • (800) 628 6364
Year founded: 1966
Ownership: Nonprofit, independent
Accreditation: Regional (North Central
    Association of Colleges and Schools)
Residency: One 3-day colloquium per semester
Cost: $$$$
Special fields: Adventure education,
    environmental education

Offers individualized M.A. programs in environmental education and adventure education. Students may take advantage of Prescott's unique nontraditional program offerings which, in the words of the school's Web site, "span the spectrum of adventure-based outdoor programming."

UNIVERSITY OF DUNDEE

Dundee DD1 4HN
United Kingdom
Web site: www.dundee.ac.uk/
    prospectus/distlearning
Email: srs@dundee.ac.uk
Phone: +44 (13) 8234 8111
Fax: +44 (13) 8234 5500
Year founded: 1981
Ownership: Nonprofit
Accreditation: Non-U.S. equivalent
Residency: None
Cost: $$$
Special fields: Medical education

The Master of Medical Education consists of six broad course module areas: assessment, curriculum development, education research, instructional materials development, special options, and teaching and learning. Students select individual units (courses) within these areas to fulfill general distribution requirements. All coursework can be completed by correspondence, and an increasing number of courses are available online.

UNIVERSITY OF IDAHO

Department of Mathematics
P.O. Box 441103
Moscow, ID 83844-1103
Web site: www.uidaho.edu/evo
Email: math@uidaho.edu
Phone: (800) 824 2889
Fax: (208) 885 5843
Year founded: 1889
Ownership: Nonprofit, state
Accreditation: Regional (Northwest
    Association of Schools and Colleges)
Residency: None
Cost: $$$
Special fields: Teaching mathematics

The Master of Arts in Teaching (M.A.T.) in mathematics education is a three-year non-thesis program designed for professional educators. The curriculum consists of ten courses, and all of them may be taken online; at the end of the program, the student must pass a three-hour written examination.

UNIVERSITY OF ILLINOIS AT CHICAGO

UIC College of Medicine
Department of Medical Education MC 591
808 South Wood Street, Floor 9
Chicago, IL 60612
Web site: www.mhpe-online.org
Phone: (312) 996 7349 • (877) 363 6656
Fax: (312) 413 2048
Email: dme-online@uic.edu
Year founded: 1891
Ownership: Nonprofit, state

Accreditation: Regional (North Central Association of Colleges and Schools)
Residency: Two 5-day summer residencies
Cost: $$$
Special fields: Health professions education

Offers an online Master of Health Professions Education addressing a wide variety of general teaching topics (instruction, assessment, leadership, and so on) as well as topics more specific to the field (such as writing for scientific publication and clinical ethics). The program can be completed in about two years.

UNIVERSITY OF MELBOURNE

Victoria, 3010
Australia
Web site: www.unimelb.edu.au/research
Email: j.gilbert@sgs.unimelb.edu.au
Phone: +61 (3) 8344 8670
Ownership: Nonprofit
Accreditation: Non-U.S. equivalent
Residency: Negotiable
Cost: $$
Special fields: Computer education, health & physical education, mathematics education

One of the most prestigious research universities in Australia, Melbourne makes its research M.Phil. programs available to students worldwide who are able to find, and work through, an approved local institution (the list of approved institutions is already fairly extensive, and students may petition to have new institutions added to the list). The program involves two to five years of study and a dissertation of about 60,000 words.

UNIVERSITY OF NORTHERN IOWA

1227 West 27th Street
Cedar Falls, IA 50614
Web site: www.uni.edu
Email: contined@uni.edu
Phone: (319) 273 2121 • (800) 772 1746
Year founded: 1847
Ownership: Nonprofit, state
Accreditation: Regional (North Central Association of Colleges and Schools)
Residency: Regional classroom meetings and on-campus summer intensives
Cost: $$$
Special fields: Communication education, middle school mathematics, music education

Offers the above programs through a combination of online study, regional extension workshops, and summer intensive seminars.

UNIVERSITY OF PRETORIA

Pretoria 0002
South Africa
Web site: www.up.ac.za/telematic
Email: telehelp@postino.up.ac.za
Phone: +27 (12) 420 3884
Fax: +27 (12) 362 5168
Year founded: 1930
Ownership: Nonprofit
Accreditation: Non-U.S. equivalent
Cost: $$
Residency: Variable
Special fields: Music education

Offers an M.Mus. in music education based on a mix of correspondence, Web-based, and on-campus study.

UNIVERSITY OF SOUTH AFRICA

P.O. Box 392
Unisa 0003
South Africa
Web site: www.unisa.ac.za
Email: study-info@unisa.ac.za
Phone: +27 (12) 429 3111
Fax: +27 (12) 429 3221
Year founded: 1873
Ownership: Nonprofit, state
Accreditation: Non-U.S. equivalent
Residency: None
Cost: $
Special fields: Health sciences education, mathematics education, natural science education

Offers an M.Ed. in the above fields. Students complete four to six intensive course modules and a thesis. All work can be completed by correspondence, though an increasing number of courses are also available online.

VIRGINIA POLYTECHNIC INSTITUTE AND STATE UNIVERSITY

Health and Physical Education Program
206 War Memorial Hall - 0313
Blacksburg, VA 24061
Web site: www.vto.vt.edu
Phone: (540) 231 5617
Fax: (540) 231 9075
Year founded: 1872
Ownership: Nonprofit, state
Accreditation: Regional (Southern Association of Colleges and Schools)
Residency: Two 2-week summer residencies
Cost: $$$
Special fields: Physical education

The M.A. in physical education can be completed almost entirely through online study, with only two

2-week summer on-campus residencies required. Students must complete nine online courses and a capstone project.

Special education

Special education involves the teaching of students with special needs; it's a broad category that includes everything from learning disabilities which may be quite mild, to moderate physical disabilities, to severe emotional disturbances. Whichever area of special education you go into, rest assured that you will need specific training in order to succeed. In fact, a growing number of states are now requiring that special education teachers earn a master's degree in the field. Other states, such as California, while not specifically requiring the M.A. or M.Ed., have so increased the requirements necessary to receive the full credential that it only makes sense for the prospective teacher to take the few additional units and earn the master's.

CHARLES STURT UNIVERSITY

International Division
Locked Bag 676
Wagga Wagga, New South Wales 2678
Australia
Web site: www.csu.edu.au
Email: inquiry@csu.edu.au
Phone: +61 (2) 6933 2666
Fax: +61 (2) 6933 2799
Year founded: 1989
Ownership: Nonprofit
Accreditation: Non-U.S. equivalent
Residency: None
Cost: $$
Special fields: Special education
The M.Ed. program in special education is available with a coursework-only track (consisting of eight course modules) and a coursework-with-project track (consisting of six modules and a capstone project). It is possible to complete either track in about two years of part-time off-campus study.

DEAKIN UNIVERSITY

Deakin International
336 Glenferrie Road
Malvern, Victoria 3144
Australia
Web site: www.deakin.edu.au

Phone: +61 (3) 9244 5095
Fax: +61 (3) 9244 5094
Year founded: 1974
Ownership: Nonprofit
Accreditation: Non-U.S. equivalent
Residency: None
Cost: $$
Special fields: Special needs education
Offers a Master of Education in special needs education. Students may choose a coursework-only track or a coursework-and-research track. The program takes two to three years to complete via part-time study.

EDITH COWAN UNIVERSITY

International Students Office
Claremont, Western Australia 6010
Australia
Web site: www.cowan.edu.au
Email: extstudi@echidna.cowan.edu.au
Phone: +61 (9) 273 8681
Year founded: 1990
Ownership: Nonprofit
Accreditation: Non-U.S. equivalent
Residency: None
Cost: $$
Special fields: Children with special needs
Offers an M.Ed., specializing in children with special needs, entirely off-campus. Students may choose a coursework-only track (comprised of eight course modules), a coursework-and-project track (comprised of six course modules and a capstone project), or a coursework-and-thesis track (comprised of four course modules and a thesis). Takes two to five years to complete.

FLINDERS UNIVERSITY

G.P.O. Box 2100
Adelaide, Southern Australia 5001
Australia
Web site: www.flinders.edu.au
Email: intl.office@flinders.edu.au
Phone: +61 (8) 201 2727 • (800) 686 3562
Fax: +61 (8) 201 3177
Year founded: 1966
Ownership: Nonprofit
Accreditation: Non-U.S. equivalent
Residency: None
Cost: $$
Special fields: Special education
The Master of Special Education is available with three possible tracks: coursework-only (consisting of 12 course modules), coursework-with-project (consisting of 10 course modules and a capstone project), and

coursework-with-thesis (consisting of 9 course modules and a thesis). Up to two-thirds of course requirements may potentially be waived on the basis of prior study and/or work experience. No residency is required.

LIBERTY UNIVERSITY

1971 University Boulevard
Lynchburg, VA 24502-2269
Web site: www.liberty.edu
Email: admissions@liberty.edu
Phone: (804) 582 2000 • (800) 424 9595
Fax: (804) 582 2304
Year founded: 1971
Ownership: Nonprofit, independent
Accreditation: Regional (Southern Association of Colleges and Schools)
Residency: Variable
Cost: $$$$
Special fields: Special education

Offers a low-residency M.Ed. in special education, designed to meet Virginia state licensure requirements. Students are required to complete four core courses, four concentration courses, and four professional courses (five for students seeking Virginia state teaching licensure). No thesis is required. Students may be required to take residential coursework in some instances.

OPEN UNIVERSITY

Walton Hall
Milton Keynes MK7 6AA
United Kingdom
Web site: www.open.ac.uk

Isadora Plunkett practicing for the video she needs to send in for her distance ethnic dance teacher course.

Email: ces-gen@open.ac.uk
Phone: +44 (190) 827 4066
Fax: +44 (190) 865 3744
Year founded: 1969
Ownership: Nonprofit
Accreditation: Non-U.S. equivalent
Residency: None
Cost: $$
Special fields: Special needs/inclusive education

The M.A. in education with emphasis in special needs and inclusive education consists of three intensive course modules. No thesis or project is required, and all coursework can be completed by correspondence.

UNIVERSITY OF MANCHESTER

School of Education
Oxford Road
Manchester M13 9PL
United Kingdom
Web site: distlearn.man.ac.uk/dl
Email: distance.admin@man.ac.uk
Phone: +44 (16) 1275 3967
Year founded: 1851
Accreditation: Non-U.S. equivalent
Ownership: Nonprofit
Residency: Usually none
Cost: $$$
Special fields: Education of the hearing impaired, profound learning disability & sensory impairment

The M.Ed. in education of the hearing impaired involves six intensive course modules and a capstone thesis of 15,000 to 20,000 words; all requirements can be completed at a distance through a mix of online and correspondence coursework. The M.S. in profound learning disability and sensory impairment mixes online study with short, intensive on-campus residencies.

UNIVERSITY OF NORTHERN IOWA

1227 West 27th Street
Cedar Falls, IA 50614
Web site: www.uni.edu
Email: contined@uni.edu
Phone: (319) 273 2121 • (800) 772 1746
Year founded: 1847
Ownership: Nonprofit, state
Accreditation: Regional (North Central Association of Colleges and Schools)
Residency: Regional classroom meetings and on-campus summer intensives
Cost: $$$
Special fields: Special education & inclusion

Offers an M.Ed. in special education and inclusion

through a combination of online study, regional extension workshops, and summer intensive seminars.

UNIVERSITY OF SOUTH AFRICA
P.O. Box 392
Unisa 0003
South Africa
Web site: www.unisa.ac.za
Email: study-info@unisa.ac.za
Phone: +27 (12) 429 3111
Fax: +27 (12) 429 3221
Year founded: 1873
Ownership: Nonprofit, state
Accreditation: Non-U.S. equivalent
Residency: None
Cost: $
Special fields: Gifted child education

Offers an M.Ed. in gifted child education. Students complete four to six intensive course modules and a thesis. All work can be completed by correspondence, though an increasing number of courses are also available online.

UNIVERSITY OF SOUTH ALABAMA
Office of Admissions
182 Administrative Building
Mobile, AL 36688-0002
Web site: usaonline.southalabama.edu
Email: admiss@usamail.usouthal.edu
Phone: (334) 460 6141 • (800) 872 5247
Fax: (334) 460 7876
Ownership: Nonprofit, state
Accreditation: Regional (Southern Association of Colleges and Schools)
Residency: None, generally
Cost: $$$
Special fields: Gifted education

Offers an M.Ed. with specialization in gifted education. This program is designed to meet Alabama state licensure requirements. All coursework can be completed online.

Interdisciplinary fields

BRUNEL UNIVERSITY
Department of Education
Uxbridge
Middlesex UB8 3PH
United Kingdom
Web site: www.brunel.ac.uk
Email: simon.bradford@brunel.ac.uk
Phone: +44 (20) 8891 0121
Fax: +44 (20) 8744 2960

Year founded: 1966
Ownership: Nonprofit
Accreditation: Non-U.S. equivalent
Residency: None
Cost: $$$
Special fields: Youth & community work

The M.A. in youth and community work consists of nine course modules that can be completed entirely by correspondence. Support is available by mail, telephone, fax, and email. No thesis is required.

CAPELLA UNIVERSITY
222 South 9th Street, 20th Floor
Minneapolis, MN 55402-3389
Web site: www.capellauniversity.edu
Email: info@capella.edu
Phone: (612) 339 8650 • (888) 227 3552
Fax: (612) 337 5396
Year founded: 1993
Ownership: Proprietary
Accreditation: Regional (North Central Association of Colleges and Schools)
Residency: Three seminars
Cost: $$$$
Special fields: School psychology

Offers an M.S. in psychology with emphasis in school psychology. Students complete five core courses, four specialization courses, three elective courses, and a capstone project. All coursework may be completed online, but students are required to attend three weekend seminars on campus.

CONCORDIA UNIVERSITY
275 Syndicate Street North
St. Paul, MN 55104
Web site: www.csp.edu/hspd
Email: cshs@csp.edu
Phone: (651) 641 8897 • (800) 211 3370
Fax: (651) 603 6144
Year founded: 1893
Ownership: Nonprofit, church
Accreditation: Regional (Middle States Association of Colleges and Schools)
Residency: One initial five-day residency
Cost: $$$
Special fields: School-age care, youth development

Offers an M.A. in education with specialization in either of the above fields. Students must attend an initial five-day residency, but all other work may be completed online. The program concludes with a capstone seminar (which must be a thesis, an appropriate portfolio, or another approved project).

Student profile: Julie Seek

Julie Seek is a 1994 graduate of the University of Tennessee at Knoxville with a Bachelor of Arts in French. Although she found her studies quite interesting, they weren't particularly practical. After graduation, she worked with several computer companies. It was while working for one of these companies, IBM, that she first visited China. From there, she moved to China to work as an English teacher. Julie is currently in the final phase of completing her M.A. degree from Azusa Pacific University. In a unique arrangement, coursework is completed in both California and Thailand while extensive homework assignments are completed in China between courses. The program takes two and a half years to complete.

Best Education Degrees: Why did you choose the institution that you did?
Julie Seek: I chose Azusa Pacific University because of its partnership with my company, English Language Institute (ELIC), in China. It offers an incredibly flexible, practical M.A. program for people who are working overseas, but who want to improve professionally. I worked for ELIC for a year and then started the M.A. program.

BED: Would you recommend this particular program to others? Why?
JS: I would recommend my program—the M.A. in TESOL from APU—because it is practical. Although I am interested in language learning theory, I like that this program focuses more on application. Since I am a teacher as well as a student, I appreciate that all that I am learning I can immediately apply

to the classroom. I have seen my teaching improve as a result of applying what I have learned in my classes.

BED: Would you recommend distance learning in general to others? Why?
JS: I would recommend distance learning for anyone who is self-motivated. Some of my classmates have commented that they have a hard time motivating themselves to get the work done, and many of my classmates have had to ask for extensions. So distance learning is not for everyone. But in general, for people who are able to motivate themselves, it is a wonderful way to get a degree!

BED: How did earning this degree enhance your career?
JS: I have not finished my degree yet, so I have not seen the benefit of the increase in salary, but that is not my primary interest anyway. The main way this degree enhanced my career has been in confirming my deep interest in TESOL. The more I learn, the more I realize I don't know, and the more I want to learn. It has also encouraged me to look into further education—a Ph.D. next!

BED: What was your primary motivation in earning this degree?
JS: I wanted to work on this degree so I would be more qualified to teach EFL (English as a foreign language). I also thought that since the program I am working on is tailored to allow me to work overseas, I could use these years in a doubly profitable way: not only to gain experience teaching overseas, but also to earn a degree that I can use almost anywhere.

FRANKLIN PIERCE LAW CENTER

Education Law Institute
2 White Street
Concord, NH 03301
Web site: www.edlaw.flpc.edu
Phone: (603) 228 1541, ext 1152
Year founded: 1973
Ownership: Nonprofit, independent
Accreditation: Regional (New England Association of Schools and Colleges) and Professional (American Bar Association)
Residency: Two summer seminars (8 days total)
Cost: $$$$
Special fields: Education law

The Master of Education Law (M.E.L.) program is a special individualized program that addresses a variety of issues pertaining to education law, conflict resolution, liability and immunity, and such. Eight courses comprise the core curriculum, along with a selection of elective courses chosen by the student and approved by the faculty. The program concludes with a capstone project or "externship" (external internship). Students have five years to complete the program.

LAKEHEAD UNIVERSITY

Graduate Studies in Education
Faculty of Education
955 Oliver Road
Thunder Bay, ON P7B 5E1
Canada
Web site: www.lakeheadu.ca
Phone: +1 (807) 343 8054
Fax: +1 (807) 346 7771
Ownership: Nonprofit
Accreditation: Non-U.S. equivalent
Residency: None
Cost: $$$
Special fields: Gerontology & education, women's studies & education

Offers an M.Ed. in the above fields by correspondence; an increasing number of courses are now also available online. Students may choose a coursework-and-thesis track (consisting of two compulsory courses, three electives, a graduate seminar, and a thesis) or a coursework-and-project track (consisting of two compulsory courses, five electives, a graduate seminar, and a project).

LIBERTY UNIVERSITY

1971 University Boulevard
Lynchburg, VA 24502-2269
Web site: www.liberty.edu
Email: admissions@liberty.edu
Phone: (804) 582 2000 • (800) 424 9595

Fax: (804) 582 2304
Year founded: 1971
Ownership: Nonprofit, independent
Accreditation: Regional (Southern Association of Colleges and Schools)
Residency: Variable
Cost: $$$$
Special fields: School counseling

Offers a low-residency M.Ed. in school counseling, in a program designed to meet Virginia state licensure requirements. Students are required to complete four core courses, seven concentration courses, and five professional courses. No thesis is required. Students may be required to take coursework in residence; in particular, all students seeking Virginia state licensure must take at least nine hours of residential coursework (though this coursework is available in a special intensive format and can be completed during summer residencies).

MONASH UNIVERSITY

Distance Education Centre
Gippsland Campus
Northways Road
Churchill, Victoria 3842
Australia
Web site: www.monash.edu.au/de
Email: course.inquiries@celts.monash.edu.au
Phone: +61 (3) 9902 6200
Fax: +61 (3) 9902 6300
Year founded: 1961
Ownership: Nonprofit
Accreditation: Non-U.S. equivalent
Residency: None
Cost: $$
Special fields: International education

Offers an M.Ed. in international education with three possible tracks: coursework-only (consisting of six course modules), coursework-and-paper (consisting of five modules and a short thesis of 10,000 words), or coursework-and-thesis (consisting of four modules and a thesis of 20,000 words). Coursework takes place primarily via correspondence (supplemented in some cases with audiocassettes); an increasing number of courses are also available online.

NOVA SOUTHEASTERN UNIVERSITY

3301 College Avenue
Fort Lauderdale, FL 33314
Web site: www.nova.edu
Email: cwis@nova.edu
Phone: (954) 262 8500 • (800) 541 6682
Year founded: 1964

Ownership: Nonprofit, independent
Accreditation: Regional (Southern Association of Colleges and Schools)
Residency: One extended weekend session per semester and annual eight-day summer residencies
Cost: $$$$
Special fields: Child & youth studies (early childhood education)

Offers an online M.S. program in child and youth studies with emphasis in early childhood education. Students must attend three to six days of extended weekend sessions each semester (held in February–March and October–November) and an eight-day summer institute (held in July or August). Students progress through the program as part of a cohort of 20–25 students. The curriculum consists of eight study areas, each including individual assignments and a capstone team project. At the end of the program, each student must complete an individual practicum (applied capstone project).

REGENT UNIVERSITY

Graduate Center
1650 Diagonal Road
Alexandria, VA 22314-2857
Web site: www.regent.edu
Email: admissions@regent.edu
Phone: (757) 226 4127 • (800) 373 5504
Fax: (703) 740 1471
Year founded: 1977
Ownership: Nonprofit, independent
Accreditation: Regional (Southern Association of Colleges and Schools)
Residency: Variable
Cost: $$$$
Special fields: School-based security & community policing

Offers a low-residency master's program in school-based security and community policing; students are required to complete ten online courses and a capstone project.

UNIVERSITY OF ILLINOIS AT URBANA-CHAMPAIGN

Urbana, IL 61801
Web site: cter.ed.uiuc.edu
Email: graduate@admissions.uiuc.edu
Phone: (217) 333 1000
Fax: (217) 333 9758
Year founded: 1867
Ownership: Nonprofit, state
Accreditation: Regional (North Central Association of Colleges and Schools)

Residency: None
Cost: $$$
Special fields: Curriculum, technology, & education reform

The online M.Ed. in curriculum, technology, and education reform involves five core courses, five elective courses, and a capstone project; students can complete the program in about three years.

UNIVERSITY OF SOUTH AFRICA

P.O. Box 392
Unisa 0003
South Africa
Web site: www.unisa.ac.za
Email: study-info@unisa.ac.za
Phone: +27 (12) 429 3111
Fax: +27 (12) 429 3221
Year founded: 1873
Ownership: Nonprofit, state
Accreditation: Non-U.S. equivalent
Residency: None
Cost: $
Special fields: Comparative education, guidance & counseling, history of education, philosophy of education, psychology of education, socio-education

Offers an M.Ed. in the above fields. Students complete four to six intensive course modules and a thesis. All work can be completed by correspondence, though an increasing number of courses are also available online.

WALDEN UNIVERSITY

155 Fifth Avenue, South
Minneapolis, MN 55401
Web site: www.waldenu.edu
Email: info@waldenu.edu
Phone: (612) 338 7224 • (800) 925 3368
Fax: (612) 338 5092
Year founded: 1970
Ownership: Nonprofit, independent
Accreditation: Regional (North Central Association of Colleges and Schools)
Residency: Extension seminars
Cost: $$$$
Special fields: Educational change & innovation

Offers an M.S. in education with specialization in educational change and innovation. This program can be completed in as little as 18 months. Students must attend seminars on a semi-regular basis; these are held at a variety of locations nationwide. The program consists of ten courses and a capstone residential seminar.

Student profile: Andrew Finch

Andrew Finch was a middle school teacher in England, then went to Korea to learn Baduk. In Seoul, he worked as an English teacher at various language institutions and Andong University. He earned his M.Ed. at Andong University before moving on to Hong Kong. He was invited back three years later to design, run, and evaluate a language program for Andong University Language Centre (this project became the subject of his Ph.D. thesis). Andrew is now Language Testing Consultant at the Hong Kong Polytechnic University.

Best Education Degrees: Why did you choose the institution that you did?
Andrew Finch: I chose Manchester University because it's in the U.K. (I am a British citizen, so things are more convenient in terms of fees) and because I saw the Distance M.Ed. advertised in the *International Guardian* newspaper. Having completed the course and having been impressed with the university and the academic staff, it seemed natural to apply for a Ph.D. with the same institution. [Ed. note: Dr. Finch completed the Ph.D., also through distance learning.]

BED: Please describe your learning experience.
AF: As a mature student (over 40) on the M.Ed., I expected to have to bite my tongue, since my teaching experience "in the trenches" would inevitably conflict with academic "theory." However, I was pleasantly surprised. The course was practically oriented and very much aware of learning issues in the classroom. Assignments were based in the classroom, and effectively made me reflect on my teaching style and principles.

BED: Would you recommend distance learning in general to others? Why?
AF: Certainly. I would always hire someone with a distance master's over someone who studied full time. Distance master's-holders have tried out all the theory in the classroom, and they know what works and what doesn't. They have been encouraged to reflect on their teaching while it happens, and they have faced the real problems that are part of the growing process. This is NOT my experience with teachers who studied only on campus.

BED: In your opinion, what type of person makes a good distance learning student?
AF: Distance students self-select. It is not easy to work through a distance course, with family and teaching commitments claiming valuable time and energy. Those who cannot apply themselves or do the reading simply drop out. Someone who has been through the mill and gained the qualification has done a heck of a lot more than simply study for a master's. He has proved his endurance, application, and sensitivity to family and work pressures.

"All right! Three more, and I'll have a cohort group."

CHAPTER 5

Earning a Certificate or Specialist Degree by Distance Learning

A teacher must believe in the value and interest of his subject as a doctor believes in health.

GILBERT HIGHET

Graduate study is not limited to those seeking master's or doctorates. Certificate programs provide the opportunity to earn graduate credit in a specialized subject without delving as deeply as a master's. The Educational Specialist (Ed.S.) degree is an interesting alternative to the doctorate. Both certificates and Ed.S.'s are available through distance learning.

The Educational Specialist (Ed.S.) Degree

The Ed.S. degree generally consists of about one year of post-master's study. It's a useful credential for teachers and administrators who would like to go a level beyond the master's, but would prefer not to pursue a doctorate. In some states, the Ed.S. puts a teacher in a higher category than those with just a master's.

As the name might imply, the Ed.S. also gives teachers the opportunity to focus on a single field—such as educational technology, administration, or curriculum design—without being saddled with the sort of general core requirements one might find in a standard Ed.D. program.

There are two limitations to the Ed.S. that should be mentioned:

1. It is designed for teachers who already hold a master's degree (although we have been told that, at some schools, it is not necessary that the master's degree actually be *in* education).

2. Although there are a few exceptions to this rule, most doctoral programs in education do not give advanced standing to holders of the Ed.S. degree; it has the reputation, by design, of being a terminal professional degree for teachers who do not plan on pursuing a doctorate in the field.

Schools Offering Educational Specialist Programs by Distance Learning

NOVA SOUTHEASTERN UNIVERSITY

3301 College Avenue
Fort Lauderdale, FL 33314
Web site: www.nova.edu
Email: cwis@nova.edu
Phone: (954) 262 8500 • (800) 541 6682
Year founded: 1964
Ownership: Nonprofit, independent
Accreditation: Regional (Southern Association of Colleges and Schools)
Cost: $$$$

Note: Although we have been told that Nova Southeastern University's highly regarded low-residency Ed.S. programs are not available as of press time, plans are in the works to make them available again soon. For the latest information, contact the school or visit the *Best Education Degrees* update page at *www.degree.net/updates/bed*.

UNIVERSITY OF SARASOTA

5250 17th Street
Sarasota, FL 34235
Web site: www.sarasota.edu
Email: uofs@embanet.com
Phone: (941) 379 0404 • (800) 331 5995
Fax: (941) 379 9464
Year founded: 1969
Ownership: Proprietary
Accreditation: Regional (Southern Association of Colleges and Schools)
Residency: Four intensive courses
Cost: $$$$
Special fields: Curriculum & instruction, educational leadership

Offers a low-residency Ed.S. in curriculum and instruction or educational leadership. Requires ten courses: four traditional, three tutorial courses, and three electives. The program concludes with a comprehensive examination. The four traditional courses must be taken in-residence at Sarasota (campuses in Sarasota and Tampa, FL, and in Orange, CA), but may be taken in a short, intensive format. Remaining coursework may be completed by distance learning. We've heard reports that the University of Sarasota may change its name to Argosy University (the school is owned by the Argosy Education Group), but the matter was still not settled when we went to press.

UNIVERSITY OF TENNESSEE AT CHATTANOOGA

Graduate Programs in Education
615 McCallie Avenue
Department 4154
Chattanooga, TN 37403-2598
Web site: www.utc.edu
Phone: (423) 755 4171
Year founded: 1886
Ownership: Nonprofit, state
Accreditation: Regional (Southern Association of Colleges and Schools)
Residency: Oral defense
Cost: $$$
Special fields: Educational technology

The Ed.S. in educational technology can be completed almost entirely through online study. Students must complete ten courses and a capstone project, and students must visit the campus for an oral defense.

VALDOSTA STATE UNIVERSITY

Department of Curriculum and Instructional
    Technology
Valdosta, GA 31698
Web site: teach.valdosta.edu/edsonline
Email: amrecess@valdosta.edu
Phone: (912) 333 5927
Year founded: 1906
Ownership: Nonprofit, state
Accreditation: Regional (Southern Association
    of Colleges and Schools)
Residency: None
Cost: $$$
Special fields: Instructional technology

The Ed.S. in instructional technology requires nine courses and a thesis. No residency is required. Applicants must have at least three years of teaching or otherwise relevant work experience to qualify; students who lack a background in instructional technology may be required to take additional supplementary coursework.

Certificates in Specific Education-Related Fields

You can be a graduate student without enrolling in a master's program. Many schools offer shorter, more focused programs in which student work is recognized by the awarding of what is generally called a certificate. You earn units just like you would in a master's program, simply not as many. There are a number of excellent reasons why a working educator might want to earn such a certificate:

▶ You would like to gain further knowledge as a teacher, but can't afford (and/or find time for) a complete degree program.

▶ You want to engage in specialized study in a field for which there are no available degree programs.

▶ You live in a state that, like California, bases its pay scale on a per-unit basis rather than per-degree.

Administration and leadership

CAPELLA UNIVERSITY

222 South 9th Street, 20th Floor
Minneapolis, MN 55402-3389
Web site: www.capellauniversity.edu
Email: info@capella.edu
Phone: (612) 339 8650 ● (888) 227 3552
Fax: (612) 337 5396
Year founded: 1993
Ownership: Proprietary
Accreditation: Regional (North Central
    Association of Colleges and Schools)
Residency: None
Cost: $$$$
Special fields: Educational administration

Online graduate certificate in educational administration.

KEELE UNIVERSITY

Postgraduate Admissions and Recruiting Office
Department of Academic Affairs
Staffordshire ST5 5BG
United Kingdom
Web site: www.keele.ac.uk
Email: aaa12@admin.keele.ac.uk

The certificate programs are organized by field of focus:

Administration and leadership	starts here
Adult and vocational education	page 81
Distance education and educational technology	page 82
Language instruction	page 84
Single subjects	page 86
Special needs	page 87
Miscellaneous programs	page 88
Foreign programs offering certificates in every subject under the sun	page 90

Phone: +44 (17) 8258 4002
Fax: +44 (17) 8263 2343
Year founded: 1949
Ownership: Nonprofit
Accreditation: Non-U.S. equivalent
Residency: None
Cost: $$$
Special fields: Effective education and
   management
Offers a postgraduate diploma in effective education and management, by correspondence.

REGENT UNIVERSITY

Graduate Center
1650 Diagonal Road
Alexandria, VA 22314-2857
Web site: www.regent.edu
Email: admissions@regent.edu
Phone: (757) 226 4127 • (800) 373 5504
Fax: (703) 740 1471
Year founded: 1977
Ownership: Nonprofit, independent
Accreditation: Regional (Southern Association
   of Colleges and Schools)
Residency: None
Cost: $$$$
Special fields: Christian school program
Online certificate in Christian school administration.

UNIVERSITY OF NORTHERN IOWA

1227 West 27th Street
Cedar Falls, IA 50614
Web site: www.uni.edu
Email: contined@uni.edu
Phone: (319) 273 2121 • (800) 772 1746
Year founded: 1847
Ownership: Nonprofit, state
Accreditation: Regional (North Central
   Association of Colleges and Schools)
Residency: On-campus summer intensives
Cost: $$$
Special fields: Principal certification
Offers a special low-residency graduate certificate program designed to fulfill Iowa state principal licensure requirements.

Adult and vocational education

BROCK UNIVERSITY

500 Glenridge Avenue
St. Catherine's, Ontario L2S 3A1
Canada
Web site: adult.ed.brocku.ca

Email: liaison@dewey.ed.brocku.ca
Phone: +1 (905) 688 5550
Year founded: 1964
Ownership: Nonprofit, state
Accreditation: Non-U.S. equivalent
Residency: None
Cost: $$$
Special fields: Adult education
Offers a five-course certificate in adult education.

CAPELLA UNIVERSITY

222 South 9th Street, 20th Floor
Minneapolis, MN 55402-3389
Web site: www.capellauniversity.edu
Email: info@capella.edu
Phone: (612) 339 8650 • (888) 227 3552
Fax: (612) 337 5396
Year founded: 1993
Ownership: Proprietary
Accreditation: Regional (North Central
   Association of Colleges and Schools)
Residency: None
Cost: $$$$
Special fields: Adult education, training &
   development
Online graduate certificate programs in the fields listed above.

GRIFFITH UNIVERSITY

Nathan
Queensland 4111
Australia
Web site: www.gu.edu.au
Email: student_enquiry@gu.edu.au
Phone: +61 (7) 3382 1339
Ownership: Nonprofit
Accreditation: Non-U.S. equivalent
Residency: None
Cost: $$
Special fields: Adult & vocational education
Undergraduate and postgraduate certificates/
diplomas in adult and vocational education, available by correspondence; a growing number of courses may also be completed online.

INDIANA UNIVERSITY

Department of Adult Education
Union Building 507
Indianapolis, IN 46202
Web site: scs.indiana.edu
Email: adulted@iupui.edu
Phone: (317) 274 3472
Fax: (317) 278 2280

Year founded: 1912
Ownership: Nonprofit, state
Accreditation: Regional (North Central
    Association of Colleges and Schools)
Residency: None
Cost: $$$
Special fields: Adult education
Online graduate certificate in adult education.

PENNSYLVANIA STATE UNIVERSITY

207 Mitchell Building
University Park, PA 16802-3601
Web site: www.outreach.psu.edu/DE
Email: psude@cde.psu.edu
Phone: (814) 865 5403 • (800) 252 3592
Fax: (814) 865 3290
Year founded: 1855
Ownership: Nonprofit, state
Accreditation: Regional (Middle States
    Association of Colleges and Schools)
Residency: None
Cost: $$$
Special fields: Adult education
Online graduate certificate in adult education.

UNIVERSITY OF SASKATCHEWAN

Extension Credit Studies
326-117 Science Place
Saskatoon, SK S7N 5C8
Canada
Web site: www.extension.usask.ca
Email: extcred@usask.ca
Phone: +1 (306) 966 5563
Fax: +1 (306) 966 5590
Year founded: 1907
Ownership: Nonprofit
Accreditation: Non-U.S. equivalent
Residency: None
Cost: $$
Special fields: Adult education
Online/correspondence-based certificate program in adult education.

UNIVERSITY OF SOUTH AUSTRALIA

G.P.O. Box 2471
Adelaide, South Australia 5001
Australia
Web site: www.unisanet.unisa.edu.au
Email: international.office@unisa.edu.au
Phone: +61 (8) 8302 0114
Fax: +61 (8) 8302 0233
Year founded: 1991
Ownership: Nonprofit
Accreditation: Non-U.S. equivalent

Residency: None
Cost: $$
Special fields: Adult & community education
Online certificate and postgraduate diploma in adult and community education.

UNIVERSITY OF SOUTHERN QUEENSLAND

International Office
Toowoomba, Queensland 4350
Australia
Web site: www.usqonline.com.au
Email: international@usq.edu.au
Phone: +61 (7) 4631 2362
Fax: +61 (7) 4636 2211
Year founded: 1967
Ownership: Nonprofit
Accreditation: Non-U.S. equivalent
Residency: None
Cost: $$
Special fields: Vocational education
Undergraduate certificate in vocational education.

VIRGINIA POLYTECHNIC INSTITUTE AND STATE UNIVERSITY

Health and Physical Education Program
206 War Memorial Hall - 0313
Blacksburg, VA 24061
Web site: www.vto.vt.edu
Phone: (540) 231 5617
Fax: (540) 231 9075
Year founded: 1872
Ownership: Nonprofit, state
Accreditation: Regional (Southern Association
    of Colleges and Schools)
Residency: None
Cost: $$$
Special fields: Career & technical education
Online certificate in career and technical education designed to meet Virginia provisional requirements for vocational educators.

Distance education and educational technology

ATHABASCA UNIVERSITY

1 University Drive
Athabasca, Alberta T9S 3A3
Canada
Web site: cde.athabascau.ca
Email: mde@athabascau.ca
Phone: (780) 675 6100 • (800) 788 9041
Fax: (780) 675 6145
Year founded: 1970

Ownership: Nonprofit
Accreditation: Non-U.S. equivalent
Residency: None
Cost: $$$
Special fields: Distance education
Offers an online advanced diploma in distance education.

CAPELLA UNIVERSITY

222 South 9th Street, 20th Floor
Minneapolis, MN 55402-3389
Web site: www.capellauniversity.edu
Email: info@capella.edu
Phone: (612) 339 8650 • (888) 227 3552
Fax: (612) 337 5396
Year founded: 1993
Ownership: Proprietary
Accreditation: Regional (North Central
    Association of Colleges and Schools)
Residency: None
Cost: $$$$
Special fields: Distance education, instructional
    design for online learning, teaching &
    training online
Online graduate certificate programs in the fields
listed above.

CALIFORNIA STATE UNIVERSITY—HAYWARD

Extended and Continuing Education
25800 Carlos Bee Boulevard
Hayward, CA 94542-3012
Web site: www.online.csuhayward.edu
Email: online@csuhayward.edu
Phone: (510) 885 3605
Fax: (510) 885 4817
Year founded: 1957
Ownership: Nonprofit, state
Accreditation: Regional (Western Association
    of Schools and Colleges)
Residency: None
Cost: $$
Special fields: Online teaching & learning
Offers a certificate in online teaching and learning.

JONES INTERNATIONAL UNIVERSITY

9697 East Mineral Avenue
Englewood, CO 80112
Web site: www.international.edu
Email: info@international.edu
Phone: (303) 784 8045 • (800) 811 5663
Fax: (303) 784 8547
Year founded: 1995
Ownership: Proprietary

Accreditation: Regional (North Central
    Association of Colleges and Schools)
Residency: None
Cost: $$$
Special fields: Distance education, educational
    technology
Online undergraduate and graduate certificates in many
distance education and educational technology fields.

MARLBORO COLLEGE

Graduate Center
28 Vernon Street, Suite 5
Brattleboro, VT 05301
Web site: www.gradcenter.marlboro.edu
Email: gradcenter@marlboro.edu
Phone: (802) 258 9200 • (888) 258 5665
Fax: (802) 258 9201
Year founded: 1946
Ownership: Nonprofit, independent
Accreditation: Regional (New England
    Association of Schools and Colleges)
Residency: Two Friday night/Saturday morning
    residencies per month
Cost: $$$$
Special fields: Teaching with Internet technologies
Offers a low-residency graduate certificate in teaching
with Internet technologies.

OPEN UNIVERSITY

Walton Hall
Milton Keynes MK7 6AA
United Kingdom
Web site: www.open.ac.uk
Email: ces-gen@open.ac.uk
Phone: +44 (19) 0827 4066
Fax: +44 (19) 0865 3744
Year founded: 1969
Ownership: Nonprofit
Accreditation: Non-U.S. equivalent
Residency: None
Cost: $$
Special fields: Open & distance education
Online graduate certificate and postgraduate diploma
in open and distance education, offered by correspondence or online study.

UNIVERSITY OF MARYLAND

University College
3501 University Boulevard, East
Adelphi, MD 20783
Web site: www.umuc.edu
Email: umucinfo@umuc.edu
Phone: (301) 985 7000 • (800) 888 8682

Fax: (301) 454 0399
Year founded: 1856
Ownership: Nonprofit, state
Accreditation: Regional (Middle States Association of Colleges and Schools)
Residency: None/low
Cost: $$$
Special fields: Distance education, educational technology

Online undergraduate and graduate diplomas in several fields related to distance education and educational technology.

UNIVERSITY OF SOUTHERN QUEENSLAND

International Office
Toowoomba, Queensland 4350
Australia
Web site: www.usqonline.com.au
Email: international@usq.edu.au
Phone: +61 (7) 4631 2362
Fax: +61 (7) 4636 2211
Year founded: 1967
Ownership: Nonprofit
Accreditation: Non-U.S. equivalent
Residency: None
Cost: $$
Special fields: Distance education, educational technology

Postgraduate diplomas in educational technology and distance education.

*"Your premise is intriguing. Your argument is flawless.
But I regret that your proposed thesis topic,
'Collecting Shiny Objects,' is not suitable for our program."*

Language instruction

ASTON UNIVERSITY

Language Studies Unit
Aston Triangle
Birmingham B4 7ET
United Kingdom
Web site: www.les.aston.ac.uk/lsu
Email: lsu@aston.ac.uk
Phone: +44 (12) 1359 3611
Fax: +44 (12) 1359 2725
Year founded: 1895
Ownership: Nonprofit
Accreditation: Non-U.S. equivalent
Residency: None
Cost: $$
Special fields: Teaching English

Certificates in the teaching of English.

CALIFORNIA STATE UNIVERSITY—FRESNO

AIC - Distance Learning
5241 N. Maple Avenue
McKee Fisk Building, Room 110
Fresno, CA 93740-8027
Web site: www.csufresno.edu/aic/distance.html
Phone: (559) 278 2058
Fax: (559) 278 7026
Year founded: 1911
Ownership: Nonprofit, state
Accreditation: Regional (Western Association of Schools and Colleges)
Residency: None
Cost: $$
Special fields: Applied linguistics/TESOL

Multiple-subject CLAD (Cross-Cultural Linguistic Academic Development) credential/certificate through off-campus study.

CALIFORNIA STATE UNIVERSITY—HAYWARD

Extended and Continuing Education
25800 Carlos Bee Boulevard
Hayward, CA 94542-3012
Web site: www.online.csuhayward.edu
Email: online@csuhayward.edu
Phone: (510) 885 3605
Fax: (510) 885 4817
Year founded: 1957
Ownership: Nonprofit, state
Accreditation: Regional (Western Association of Schools and Colleges)
Residency: None
Cost: $$
Special fields: Spanish for teachers

Offers an online CLAD (Cross-Cultural Linguistic Academic Development) certificate in Spanish, designed specifically for teachers.

EMPORIA STATE UNIVERSITY

1200 Commercial
Box 4052
Emporia, KS 66801-5087
Web site: lifelong.emporia.edu
Email: lifelong@emporia.edu
Phone: (316) 341 5385
Fax: (316) 341 5744
Year founded: 1863
Ownership: Nonprofit, state
Accreditation: Regional (North Central Association of Colleges and Schools)
Cost: $$$
Special fields: English as a Second Language (ESL)
Offers an online endorsement program in ESL for teachers who work with students who speak English as a second language.

FLORIDA GULF COAST UNIVERSITY

Distance Learning Program
10501 FGCU Boulevard
Fort Myers, FL 33908-4500
Web site: www.fgcu.edu/DL
Email: tdugas@fgcu.edu
Phone: (941) 590 2315
Year founded: 1997
Ownership: Nonprofit
Accreditation: Regional (Southern Association of Colleges and Schools)
Residency: None
Cost: $$$
Special fields: English as a Second Language (ESL)
Offers an online ESL endorsement for K–12 teachers.

NEW SCHOOL UNIVERSITY

68 Fifth Avenue
New York, NY 10011
Web site: www.dialnsa.edu
Email: admissions@dialnsa.edu
Phone: (212) 229 5880
Fax: (212) 989 2928
Year founded: 1919
Ownership: Nonprofit, independent
Accreditation: Regional (Middle States Association of Colleges and Schools)
Residency: None
Cost: $$$
Special fields: TESOL (Teachers of English to Students of Other Languages)
Offers an online certificate program in TESOL.

OPEN UNIVERSITY

Walton Hall
Milton Keynes MK7 6AA
United Kingdom
Web site: www.open.ac.uk
Email: ces-gen@open.ac.uk
Phone: +44 (19) 0827 4066
Fax: +44 (19) 0865 3744
Year founded: 1969
Ownership: Nonprofit
Accreditation: Non-U.S. equivalent
Residency: None
Cost: $$
Special fields: Language & literacy education
Postgraduate diploma in language and literacy education, through correspondence or online study.

REGENT UNIVERSITY

Graduate Center
1650 Diagonal Road
Alexandria, VA 22314-2857
Web site: www.regent.edu
Email: admissions@regent.edu
Phone: (757) 226 4127 • (800) 373 5504
Fax: (703) 740 1471
Year founded: 1977
Ownership: Nonprofit, independent
Accreditation: Regional (Southern Association of Colleges and Schools)
Residency: None
Cost: $$$$
Special fields: TESOL (Teachers of English to Students of Other Languages)
Online certificate in TESOL.

UNIVERSITY OF LEICESTER

University Road
Leicester LE1 7RH
United Kingdom
Web site: www.le.ac.uk
Email: higherdegrees@le.ac.uk
Phone: +44 (11) 6252 2298
Fax: +44 (11) 6252 2200
Year founded: 1921
Ownership: Nonprofit
Accreditation: Non-U.S. equivalent
Residency: None
Cost: $$$
Special fields: TESOL (Teachers of English to Students of Other Languages)
Postgraduate diploma in TESOL.

UNIVERSITY OF MANCHESTER

School of Education
Oxford Road
Manchester M13 9PL
United Kingdom
Web site: distlearn.man.ac.uk/dl
Email: distance.admin@man.ac.uk
Phone: +44 (16) 1275 3967
Year founded: 1851
Ownership: Nonprofit
Accreditation: Non-U.S. equivalent
Residency: Usually none
Cost: $$$
Special fields: English language teaching
Online/correspondence-based postgraduate diploma in English language teaching.

UNIVERSITY OF SASKATCHEWAN

Extension Credit Studies
326-117 Science Place
Saskatoon, SK S7N 5C8
Canada
Web site: www.extension.usask.ca
Email: extcred@usask.ca
Phone: +1 (306) 966 5563
Fax: +1 (306) 966 5590
Year founded: 1907
Ownership: Nonprofit
Accreditation: Non-U.S. equivalent
Residency: None
Cost: $$
Special fields: TESOL (Teachers of English to Students of Other Languages)
Online/correspondence-based certificate program in TESOL.

UNIVERSITY OF TEXAS

Office of Information Technology and Distance Education
201 West Seventh Street
Austin, TX 78701
Web site: www.telecampus.utsystem.edu
Email: telecampus@utsystem.edu
Phone: (512) 499 4207 • (888) 786 9832
Year founded: 1973
Ownership: Nonprofit, state
Accreditation: Regional (Southern Association of Colleges and Schools)
Residency: None
Cost: $$
Special fields: English as a Second Language (ESL)
An online ESL endorsement program for teachers.

Single subjects

GLOBAL UNIVERSITY OF THE ASSEMBLIES OF GOD

1211 S. Glenstone Avenue
Springfield, MO 65804
Web site: www.globaluniversity.edu
Email: sgs@globaluniversity.edu
Phone: (800) 443 1083
Fax: (417) 862 0863
Year founded: 2000
Ownership: Nonprofit, church
Accreditation: DETC (Distance Education and Training Council)
Residency: None
Cost: $$$
Special fields: Christian education
Online and correspondence-based certificates in religious education.

GRIGGS UNIVERSITY

12501 Old Columbia Pike
Silver Spring, MD 20904-6600
Web site: www.griggs.edu
Phone: (301) 680 6570 • (800) 782 4769
Fax: (301) 680 5157
Year founded: 1909
Ownership: Nonprofit, church
Accreditation: Distance Education and Training Council (DETC)
Residency: None
Cost: $$
Special fields: Religious education
Undergraduate certificate in religious education, entirely by correspondence or online study.

UNIVERSITY OF DUNDEE

Dundee DD1 4HN
United Kingdom
Web site: www.dundee.ac.uk/ prospectus/distlearning
Email: srs@dundee.ac.uk
Phone: +44 (13) 8234 8111
Fax: +44 (13) 8234 5500
Year founded: 1981
Ownership: Nonprofit
Accreditation: Non-U.S. equivalent
Residency: None
Cost: $$$
Special fields: Medical education
Online postgraduate diploma in medical education.

UNIVERSITY OF GLASGOW

22 Western Court
Glasgow G12 8SQ
United Kingdom
Web site: www.gla.ac.uk/Inter/GUIDE
Email: guide@mis.gla.ac.uk
Phone: +44 (14) 1330 3870
Fax: +44 (14) 1330 4079
Year founded: 1451
Ownership: Nonprofit
Accreditation: Non-U.S. equivalent
Residency: None
Cost: $$$
Special fields: Religious education

Correspondence-based postgraduate diploma in religious education.

UNIVERSITY OF SASKATCHEWAN

Extension Credit Studies
326-117 Science Place
Saskatoon, SK S7N 5C8
Canada
Web site: www.extension.usask.ca
Email: extcred@usask.ca
Phone: +1 (306) 966 5563
Fax: +1 (306) 966 5590
Year founded: 1907
Ownership: Nonprofit
Accreditation: Non-U.S. equivalent
Residency: None
Cost: $$
Special fields: Ecological education

Online/correspondence-based certificate program in ecological education.

Special needs

EMPORIA STATE UNIVERSITY

1200 Commercial
Box 4052
Emporia, KS 66801-5087
Web site: lifelong.emporia.edu
Email: lifelong@emporia.edu
Phone: (316) 341 5385
Fax: (316) 341 5744
Year founded: 1863
Ownership: Nonprofit, state
Accreditation: Regional (North Central Association of Colleges and Schools)
Cost: $$$
Special fields: Early childhood special education

Offers an endorsement in early childhood special education, through a mix of online study and on-campus intensives.

OPEN UNIVERSITY

Walton Hall
Milton Keynes MK7 6AA
United Kingdom
Web site: www.open.ac.uk
Email: ces-gen@open.ac.uk
Phone: +44 (19) 0827 4066
Fax: +44 (19) 0865 3744
Year founded: 1969
Ownership: Nonprofit
Accreditation: Non-U.S. equivalent
Residency: None
Cost: $$
Special fields: Co-ordination of special education, special needs in education

Postgraduate certificate in co-ordination of special education, and postgraduate diploma in special needs in education.

UNIVERSITY OF BIRMINGHAM

Edgbaston
Birmingham B15 2TT
United Kingdom
Web site: www.edu.bham.ac.uk/CPD
Email: d.eaton@bham.ac.uk
Phone: +44 (12) 1414 4856
Year founded: 1900
Ownership: Nonprofit
Accreditation: Non-U.S. equivalent
Residency: None
Cost: $$$
Special fields: Special education

Online postgraduate diploma in special education.

UNIVERSITY OF MANCHESTER

School of Education
Oxford Road
Manchester M13 9PL
United Kingdom
Web site: distlearn.man.ac.uk/dl
Email: distance.admin@man.ac.uk
Phone: +44 (16) 1275 3967
Year founded: 1851
Ownership: Nonprofit
Accreditation: Non-U.S. equivalent
Residency: Usually none
Cost: $$$
Special fields: Education of the hearing impaired

Low-residency postgraduate diploma in education of the hearing impaired.

UNIVERSITY OF SOUTH ALABAMA

Office of Admissions
182 Administrative Building
Mobile, AL 36688-0002
Web site: usaonline.southalabama.edu
Email: admiss@usamail.usouthal.edu
Phone: (334) 460 6141 • (800) 872 5247
Fax: (334) 460 7876
Ownership: Nonprofit, state
Accreditation: Regional (Southern Association
    of Colleges and Schools)
Residency: None, generally
Cost: $$$
Special fields: Gifted education
Online graduate certificate in gifted education.

Miscellaneous programs

CAPELLA UNIVERSITY

222 South 9th Street, 20th Floor
Minneapolis, MN 55402-3389
Web site: www.capellauniversity.edu
Email: info@capella.edu
Phone: (612) 339 8650 • (888) 227 3552
Fax: (612) 337 5396
Year founded: 1993
Ownership: Proprietary
Accreditation: Regional (North Central
    Association of Colleges and Schools)
Residency: None
Cost: $$$$
Special fields: School psychology
Certificate in school psychology can be completed
entirely online.

CONCORDIA UNIVERSITY

275 Syndicate Street North
St. Paul, MN 55104
Web site: www.csp.edu/hspd
Email: cshs@csp.edu
Phone: (651) 641 8897 • (800) 211 3370
Fax: (651) 603 6144
Year founded: 1893
Ownership: Nonprofit, church
Accreditation: Regional (Middle States
    Association of Colleges and Schools)
Residency: One initial five-day residency
Cost: $$$
Special fields: Early childhood education
Online certificate in early childhood education.

EMPORIA STATE UNIVERSITY

1200 Commercial
Box 4052
Emporia, KS 66801-5087
Web site: lifelong.emporia.edu
Email: lifelong@emporia.edu
Phone: (316) 341 5385
Fax: (316) 341 5744
Year founded: 1863
Ownership: Nonprofit, state
Accreditation: Regional (North Central
    Association of Colleges and Schools)
Cost: $$$
Special fields: Early childhood special education
Offers an endorsement in early childhood special edu-
cation, through a mix of online study and on-campus
intensives.

FRANKLIN PIERCE LAW CENTER

Education Law Institute
2 White Street
Concord, NH 03301
Web site: www.edlaw.flpc.edu
Phone: (603) 228 1541, ext 1152
Year founded: 1973
Ownership: Nonprofit, independent
Accreditation: Regional (New England
    Association of Schools and Colleges)
    and Professional (American Bar Association)
Residency: Two summer seminars (eight days total)
Cost: $$$$
Special fields: Education law
Offers a low-residency Certificate of Advanced Gradu-
ate Study (CAGS) in education law.

OPEN UNIVERSITY

Walton Hall
Milton Keynes MK7 6AA
United Kingdom
Web site: www.open.ac.uk
Email: ces-gen@open.ac.uk
Phone: +44 (19) 0827 4066
Fax: +44 (19) 0865 3744
Year founded: 1969
Ownership: Nonprofit
Accreditation: Non-U.S. equivalent
Residency: None
Cost: $$
Special fields: Child development, continuing
    professional development, professional
    studies in education, teaching & learning
    in higher education
Postgraduate diplomas in child development and pro-
fessional studies in education, and graduate certificates

in continuing professional development, professional studies in education, and teaching and learning in higher education. All coursework can be completed online or via correspondence.

UNIVERSITY OF SOUTH ALABAMA

Office of Admissions
182 Administrative Building
Mobile, AL 36688-0002
Web site: usaonline.southalabama.edu
Email: admiss@usamail.usouthal.edu
Phone: (334) 460 6141 • (800) 872 5247
Fax: (334) 460 7876
Ownership: Nonprofit, state
Accreditation: Regional (Southern Association of Colleges and Schools)
Residency: None, generally
Cost: $$$
Special fields: Collaborative teacher education
Graduate certificate in collaborative teacher education.

UNIVERSITY OF SOUTH AUSTRALIA

G.P.O. Box 2471
Adelaide, South Australia 5001
Australia
Web site: www.unisanet.unisa.edu.au
Email: international.office@unisa.edu.au
Phone: +61 (8) 8302 0114
Fax: +61 (8) 8302 0233
Year founded: 1991
Ownership: Nonprofit
Accreditation: Non-U.S. equivalent
Residency: None
Cost: $$
Special fields: Early childhood education
Online certificates/postgraduate diplomas in early childhood education.

UNIVERSITY OF SOUTHERN QUEENSLAND

International Office
Toowoomba, Queensland 4350
Australia
Web site: www.usqonline.com.au
Email: international@usq.edu.au
Phone: +61 (7) 4631 2362
Fax: +61 (7) 4636 2211
Year founded: 1967
Ownership: Nonprofit
Accreditation: Non-U.S. equivalent
Residency: None
Cost: $$
Special fields: Education studies
Undergraduate certificate in education studies.

UNIVERSITY OF TEXAS

Office of Information Technology and Distance Education
201 West Seventh Street
Austin, TX 78701
Web site: www.telecampus.utsystem.edu
Email: telecampus@utsystem.edu
Phone: (512) 499 4207 • (888) 786 9832
Year founded: 1973
Ownership: Nonprofit, state
Accreditation: Regional (Southern Association of Colleges and Schools)
Residency: None
Cost: $$
Special fields: Chess in education
An online certificate dealing with chess as an educational tool.

UNIVERSITY OF WISCONSIN—MILWAUKEE

School of Library and Information Science
P.O. Box 413
Milwaukee, WI 53211
Web site: www.slis.uwm.edu
Email: info@slis.uwm.edu
Phone: (414) 229 4707 • (888) 349 3432
Fax: (414) 229 4848
Year founded: 1885
Ownership: Nonprofit, state
Accreditation: Regional (North Central Association of Colleges and Schools) and Professional (American Library Association)
Residency: None
Cost: $$$
Special fields: Library science
Online certificate equivalent to 901/902 Online Wisconsin School Library Media Specialist Certification.

UNIVERSITY OF WYOMING

Department of Adult Learning and Technology
P.O. Box 3374, Education Building, Room 1
Laramie, WY 82071-3374
Web site: ecampus.uwyo.edu
Phone: (307) 766 3247
Year founded: 1886
Ownership: Nonprofit, state
Accreditation: Regional (North Central Association of Colleges and Schools)
Residency: One week
Cost: $$$
Special fields: Early childhood education
Online certificate for early childhood program directors.

More fields than you can shake a hickory stick at

The following non-U.S. schools, all of them south of the equator, offer a vast array of certificate programs in a vast array of fields—far more than we have space to list, in fact. They are worth checking out.

Note: Internationally, a "diploma" is awarded for a graduate program that is roughly halfway between a certificate and a master's degree.

CENTRAL QUEENSLAND UNIVERSITY
Australia
www.cqu.edu.au
Certificates and diplomas in dozens of fields. Some programs can be completed entirely off-campus, while others may require brief intensive workshop sessions.

CHARLES STURT UNIVERSITY
Australia
www.csu.edu.au
Many, many certificate and diploma programs. Most can be completed through online or correspondence-based study, but a few require on-campus time.

During the seventh hour of Desert Island University's elaborate nine-hour commencement ceremony, Chancellor Morganstern begins to wish he had rented an auditorium with restroom facilities.

CURTIN UNIVERSITY OF TECHNOLOGY
Australia
www.curtin.edu.au
Certificates and diplomas. Some can be completed entirely by distance learning, but quite a few may require students to attend on-campus workshops.

EDITH COWAN UNIVERSITY
Australia
www.cowan.edu.au
Scores of certificate and diploma programs in education-related fields, ranging from Japanese language instruction to religious education to guidance counseling. Most can be completed entirely by correspondence or online study.

FLINDERS UNIVERSITY
Australia
www.flinders.edu.au
Certificate and diploma programs in an array of fields, including special education and early childhood studies.

MONASH UNIVERSITY
Australia
www.monash.edu
One of the largest universities in Australia. Certificates and diplomas in a vast array of fields through off-campus study and/or short intensive on-campus residency sessions.

NORTHERN TERRITORY UNIVERSITY
Australia
www.ntu.edu.au
Certificates and diploma programs in an array of fields.

UNIVERSITY OF SOUTH AFRICA
South Africa
www.unisa.ac.za
Literally hundreds of certificate and diploma programs, including dozens that seem to be designed to meet some South African teacher licensure requirements.

CHAPTER 6

Earning a Doctorate in Education by Distance Learning

In examinations, the foolish ask questions that the wise cannot answer.
OSCAR WILDE

A doctorate in education is typically used to become a professor of education, working at the college level to teach people how to teach. For educators drawn to the frontier of their profession—publishing research and sharing wisdom with the next generation of teachers—academia can provide an invigorating career.

Be forewarned, however, that full-time professorships are increasingly hard to come by. The current trend at colleges and universities within the U.S. is to hire fewer tenure-track professors and to hire more adjunct (part-time) faculty. The advantage to the student is that often the adjunct faculty are still in the public school classroom. The disadvantage is that, for those who wish to be professors of education, there are fewer opportunities. By the way, this trend runs through most of academia. It's tough to get one of these jobs.

Fortunately, there is demand for doctors of education beyond the college campus. In fact, in the local school district and in the business world, a doctorate will distinguish you from the crowd and open up exciting job opportunities, while in academia you are just another Ph.D.

If, for example, your goal is to be an administrator within a school district, your odds increase exponentially if you have a doctorate. You will find few superintendents these days who do not have doctorates. In some districts, many of the school principals have doctorates.

Another possibility is to become the curriculum coordinator for a public school district. This person is primarily responsible for what is taught in the classroom and is in charge of implementing the state frameworks for each curricular area. Almost without exception, this position requires a significant number of years of teaching, plus a graduate degree.

In the private sector, professional educators are getting jobs as corporate trainers. It is becoming increasingly common for industry to hire people with doctorates because they often have the requisite skills to succeed. While this has been true for science graduates for a while, it is becoming increasingly true for those in the humanities. This is particularly true in places with low unemployment. (The Silicon Valley of California is rife with former teachers who now work for tech companies.)

The publishing industry, particularly educational publishers, are always looking for people who can not only be editors, but who understand in detail the educational field. Again, your having a doctorate in the field can be seen as a huge advantage for the company, not only in prestige, but in the knowledge which you bring to the table.

And let us not fail to mention earning a doctorate for the pure love of learning, or to be the best educator you possibly can. Sure, it may seem like overkill for a fifth grade teacher to have a Ph.D., but in some states, a doctorate puts you in the highest possible licensure bracket as a teacher (and at the top of the salary range). This is certainly the case in Mississippi, where only doctorate-holding teachers can advance to the prestigious AAAA certification level.

Earning a doctorate at a distance

In the United States, the distance-learning doctorate is still a rarity. At press time, only one school—Touro University International, a branch of New York's Touro College—publicly offers 100% online Ph.D.'s, and even Touro doesn't offer any in education. All of the U.S.-based programs listed in this chapter require residency of some kind, though some of them don't require very much. For example, students in Liberty University's Ed.D. program spend only two weeks on campus per year in an intensive residency session that can be taken during the summer.

In the United Kingdom, South Africa, and Australia, the game is a little different because they use a purely research-oriented doctorate model. While doctoral students in the U.S. complete 15 to 20 courses before moving on to a capstone dissertation, students in Commonwealth countries jump right to the dissertation (which is usually longer and more involved than a U.S. dissertation). Most universities allow students to do their dissertation research off-campus. This doesn't mean that some residency isn't required, but it's usually negotiated by the relevant faculty members and on a case-by-case basis.

Some students may prefer a U.S.-model doctorate, while others might prefer a Commonwealth-model doctorate. For this reason, we've divided the listings in this chapter into two sections: one listing coursework-based doctoral programs (starting here), and the other listing research-based doctoral programs (starting on page 96).

Ph.D. vs. Ed.D.

There are two basic types of doctorates in education: the Doctor of Education (Ed.D.) and the Doctor of Philosophy in Education (Ph.D.). The theory behind the difference is that the Ed.D. is a practitioner's credential (superintendents, principals, etc.) and the Ph.D. is the academic's credential (professors). This line, however, has become increasingly blurred over the years. It is now possible to find many university professors who possess Ed.D.'s and many superintendents who have Ph.D.'s. If the content of a particular program matches your needs, don't worry about the initials that come with it. Whether it is an Ed.D. or a Ph.D. makes little difference within the education field.

Schools Offering Low-Residency Education-Related Doctorates Through a Mix of Coursework and Research

CAPELLA UNIVERSITY

222 South 9th Street, 20th Floor
Minneapolis, MN 55402-3389
Web site: www.capellauniversity.edu
Email: info@capella.edu
Phone: (612) 339 8650 • (888) 227 3552
Fax: (612) 337 5396
Year founded: 1993
Ownership: Proprietary
Accreditation: Regional (North Central Association of Colleges and Schools)
Residency: Two 1-week seminars, three or more 2–3 day seminars
Cost: $$$$
Special fields: Adult education, education (general), elementary & secondary educational administration, higher educational administration, instructional design for online learning, teaching & learning

Offers a Ph.D. in education with optional specialization in the fields listed above. Most study takes place online. Students in the Ph.D. program complete 9 core courses, 16 elective courses, a comprehensive examination, and a dissertation.

FIELDING INSTITUTE

2122 Santa Barbara Street
Santa Barbara, CA 93105
Web site: www.fielding.edu
Email: admissions@fielding.edu
Phone: (805) 687 1099 • (800) 340 1099
Year founded: 1974
Ownership: Nonprofit, independent
Accreditation: Regional (Western Association of Schools and Colleges)
Residency: Five-day admissions workshop
Cost: $$$$
Special fields: Educational leadership & change

The Ed.D. in educational leadership and change involves eight online courses, a comprehensive examination, and a dissertation. Five-course specialization tracks are available in administration and policy, interaction and development, power and change, and teaching and learning. The program can be completed in as little as two years, but usually takes longer.

Key to listings

NAME OF SCHOOL
Postal Address (*United States if country not specified*)
Web site URL
Email address
Phone • Tollfree phone (*If a U.S. number, country code (+1) not included*)
Fax
Year founded
Ownership Proprietary or nonprofit (state, independent, or church)
Accreditation Type of accreditation (regional, national, or non-U.S. equivalent) and responsible agency. All schools listed in this book have proper accreditation. See Appendix C for a more thorough explanation of this concept.
Residency Amount of on-campus attendance required
Cost Subjective interpretation of school's relative cost: $ (dirt cheap) to $$$$$ (expensive)
Special fields Fields of study, if other than general education
Description Specific information on the school's offerings

LIBERTY UNIVERSITY

1971 University Boulevard
Lynchburg, VA 24502-2269
Web site: www.liberty.edu
Email: admissions@liberty.edu
Phone: (804) 582 2000 • (800) 424 9595
Fax: (804) 582 2304
Year founded: 1971
Ownership: Nonprofit, independent
Accreditation: Regional (Southern Association of Colleges and Schools)
Residency: Two weeks per year
Cost: $$$$
Special fields: Educational leadership

The Liberty Ed.D. in educational leadership involves 12 online courses, a comprehensive examination, and a dissertation. Four of the 12 courses are drawn from a core list; the other 8 constitute a specialization track in administration, curriculum, or instruction.

NOVA SOUTHEASTERN UNIVERSITY

3301 College Avenue
Fort Lauderdale, FL 33314
Web site: www.nova.edu
Email: cwis@nova.edu
Phone: (954) 262 8500 • (800) 541 6682
Year founded: 1964
Ownership: Nonprofit, independent
Accreditation: Regional (Southern Association
of Colleges and Schools)
Residency: Two- to three-day regional monthly
meetings and two 1-week residency sessions
Cost: $$$
Special fields: Adult education, child & youth
studies, computing & information technol-
ogy, computing technology in education,
educational leadership, health care education,
higher education, instructional technology &
distance education, vocational/technological/
occupational education

Offers a Ph.D. in computing technology in education,
and an Ed.D. in the other fields listed above. The pro-
gram follows a cohort model wherein 20–25 students
meet monthly and progress through the program at
about the same pace, and generally takes about three
years to complete.

OPEN UNIVERSITY OF HONG KONG

30 Good Shepherd Street
Ho Man Tin, Kowloon, Hong Kong
Web site: www.ouhk.edu.hk
Email: regwww@ouhk.edu.hk
Phone: +852 2768 6000
Fax: +852 2715 0760
Year founded: 1989
Ownership: Nonprofit
Accreditation: Non-U.S. equivalent
Cost: $$

Offers a general Ed.D. through a mix of coursework
and research. Students must submit a research
proposal at the beginning of the program, and may be
asked to visit the campus for an interview. Instruction
is in English and Chinese.

PEPPERDINE UNIVERSITY

24255 Pacific Coast Highway
Malibu, CA 90263
Web site: www.pepperdine.edu
Email: admission-seaver@pepperdine.edu
Phone: (310) 456 4000
Fax: (310) 456 4357
Year founded: 1937

Ownership: Nonprofit, independent
Accreditation: Regional (Western Association
of Schools and Colleges)
Residency: Five short residencies per year
(see below)
Cost: $$$$
Special fields: Educational technology

The Ed.D. in educational technology involves 13 online
courses, a comprehensive examination, and a doctoral
dissertation. Students are required to attend five face-
to-face sessions each year: four are weekend residencies, but at least one must be a one-week intensive.
Sessions are held in Los Angeles; Washington, DC; and
London. The program can be completed in three to
five years.

PURDUE UNIVERSITY

West Lafayette, IN 47907
Web site: distance.soe.purdue.edu
Phone: (765) 494 1776
Fax: (765) 494 0544
Year founded: 1869
Ownership: Nonprofit, state
Accreditation: Regional (North Central
Association of Colleges and Schools)
Residency: Short
Cost: $$$$$
Special fields: Educational administration
(educational foundations, higher education,
K–12 education)

The Ph.D. program in educational administration is
available with specialization tracks in educational
foundations, higher education, and K–12 education.
Students progress through the program with a group
of 20–25 other students, attending a regular series of
online meetings and completing coursework at roughly
the same pace. The program can be completed in
about three years.

SOUTHERN BAPTIST THEOLOGICAL SEMINARY

2825 Lexington Road
Louisville, KY 40280
Web site: www.sbts.edu
Phone: (502) 897 4011 • (800) 626 5525
Fax: (502) 897 4880
Year founded: 1859
Ownership: Nonprofit, church
Accreditation: Regional (Southern Association
of Colleges and Schools)
Residency: Three seminars per year
Cost: $$$$
Special fields: Educational leadership

The Ed.D. in leadership is based on a cohort model; a group of 20–25 students progresses through the program at roughly the same pace, meeting on-campus three times per year for seminars. The remainder of the work is completed online. The curriculum addresses seven areas of study: history and philosophy of education, leadership, practice of education, psychology and sociology of education, research, teaching and learning, and theology. A dissertation is required. The program can be completed in three years.

TEXAS A&M UNIVERSITY—COMMERCE

P.O. Box 3011
Commerce, TX 75429
Web site: www.tamu-commerce.edu/coe/
psy/Psyphd.htm
Email: dean_ginther@tamu-commerce.edu
Phone: (903) 886 5102
Fax: (903) 886 5888
Year founded: 1889
Ownership: Nonprofit, state
Accreditation: Regional (Southern Association of Colleges and Schools)
Cost: $$$
Special fields: Educational psychology

At press time, about 60% of the required courses for the Ph.D. in educational psychology had been placed online. More are added each semester, and it's expected that the program will be adapted to an almost 100% online format within the near future. Students are required to complete 24 courses, a dissertation, and appropriate field work. The program can be completed in three years.

UNION INSTITUTE

440 East McMillan Street
Cincinnati, OH 45206-1925
Web site: www.tui.edu
Email: admission@tui.edu
Phone: (513) 861 6400 • (800) 486 3116
Fax: (513) 861 0779
Year founded: 1964
Ownership: Nonprofit, independent
Accreditation: Regional (North Central Association of Colleges and Schools)
Residency: Short residencies totaling 30–35 days
Cost: $$$$$

Offers a student-defined, interdisciplinary Ph.D. in virtually any field of study; each student works with a hand-picked committee to design a suitable program in the student's field of choice, provided that it can be accommodated. Each student completes modules in an individualized learning contract, attends her choice of five-day seminars held at locations worldwide, and completes an original Project Demonstrating Excellence (PDE), which can be a traditional dissertation, a suitable novel, a supervised community project, or another equivalent capstone work. The entire program can be completed in two years, although three to five years is a more reasonable estimate.

UNIVERSIDAD NACIONAL DE EDUCACION A DISTANCIA

Calle Conde de Penalver 38, 3rd Floor
Madrid 28006
Spain
Web site: www.uned.es
Phone: +34 (1) 398 6545
Fax: +34 (1) 398 8086
Year founded: 1972
Ownership: Nonprofit
Accreditation: Non-U.S. equivalent
Residency: Short residency at regional center
Cost: $$

UNED offers a low-residency doctorate in education based on a mix of coursework and independent research. Students must attend a few face-to-face sessions, but need not actually travel to Spain to do so. UNED has study centers in nine countries, including the U.S. (New York) and Mexico. The UNED doctorate in education can be tailored to a number of different specialization tracks. Instruction is in Spanish.

"When you sign up for our program, someday you'll hear the message 'You've got yourself an Ed.D., good buddy.' "

UNIVERSITY OF MONTANA

Missoula, MT 59812
Web site: www.umt.edu/ccesp
Email: ckelly@selway.umt.edu
Phone: (406) 243 0211 • (800) 462 8636
Fax: (406) 243 2797
Year founded: 1893
Ownership: Nonprofit, state
Accreditation: Regional (Northwestern
    Association of Schools and Colleges)
Residency: Six weekends each semester
    and three weeks over the summer
Cost: $$$
Special fields: Educational leadership

The Ed.D. in educational leadership involves 21 courses, a comprehensive examination, and a dissertation. A substantial amount of on-campus residency is required. The program can be completed in three years.

UNIVERSITY OF NEBRASKA—LINCOLN

334 Nebraska Center
Lincoln, NE 68583-9805
Web site: dcs.unl.edu
Email: jgunn2@unl.edu
Phone: (402) 472 6550
Fax: (402) 472 1901
Year founded: 1869
Ownership: Nonprofit, state
Accreditation: Regional (North Central
    Association of Colleges and Schools)
Residency: Two 5-week summer residencies
Cost: $$$
Special fields: Administration, curriculum,
    & instruction

Offers Ed.D. and Ph.D. programs in administration, curriculum, and instruction through online study and two-way video. A group of students progresses through the program at roughly the same pace, finishing up in about three years. A dissertation is required.

WALDEN UNIVERSITY

155 Fifth Avenue, South
Minneapolis, MN 55401
Web site: www.waldenu.edu
Email: info@waldenu.edu
Phone: (612) 338 7224 • (800) 925 3368
Fax: (612) 338 5092
Year founded: 1970
Ownership: Nonprofit, independent
Accreditation: Regional (North Central
    Association of Colleges and Schools)

Residency: Variable
Cost: $$$$

Offers an individualized Ph.D. in education. After designing and submitting for faculty approval a Professional Development Plan, students complete a series of contract-based learning modules instead of formal coursework. A dissertation is required. The program can be tailored to the specific interests of virtually any student working within the field of education.

Schools Offering Doctorates by Research

AUSTRALIAN CATHOLIC UNIVERSITY

International Education Office
P.O. Box 968
North Sydney, New South Wales 2059
Australia
Web site: www.acu.edu.au
Email: international@acu.edu.au
Phone: +61 (2) 9739 2072
Fax: +61 (2) 9739 2001
Year founded: 1991
Ownership: Nonprofit
Accreditation: Non-U.S. equivalent
Residency: Negotiable
Cost: $$

Offers a research-based Ed.D. that can, on a case-by-case basis, be negotiated to a low-residency or no-residency format. Some preliminary courses on research methods may be required.

Special Note on Research Doctorates

Students generally begin a traditional U.S. doctoral dissertation by applying to the program, establishing faculty contacts, and then developing a research proposal. When applying to a research doctorate program, it is usually more effective to do the reverse: decide on a strong research topic, email a faculty member explaining the topic and your desire to study with minimal on-campus residency, and *then* apply to the university with the blessings of the faculty member.

EDITH COWAN UNIVERSITY

International Students Office
Claremont, Western Australia 6010
Australia
Web site: www.cowan.edu.au
Email: extstudi@echidna.cowan.edu.au
Phone: +61 (9) 273 8681
Year founded: 1990
Ownership: Nonprofit
Accreditation: Non-U.S. equivalent
Cost: $$
Special fields: Applied linguistics

Offers research-based Ph.D. programs in education and applied linguistics. Each program involves three to six years of part-time external research culminating in a dissertation of about 100,000 words.

FLINDERS UNIVERSITY

G.P.O. Box 2100
Adelaide, South Australia 5001
Australia
Web site: www.flinders.edu.au
Email: intl.office@flinders.edu.au
Phone: +61 (8) 201 2727 • (800) 686 3562
Fax: +61 (8) 201 3177
Year founded: 1966
Ownership: Nonprofit
Accreditation: Non-U.S. equivalent
Cost: $$

Offers a research-based Ph.D. in education. Residency is negotiated on a case-by-case basis. The program can be completed in three to six years of part-time study.

MACQUARIE UNIVERSITY

Centre for Open Education
Building X5B
Sydney, New South Wales 2109
Australia
Web site: www.coe.mq.edu.au
Email: coe@mq.edu.au
Phone: +61 (2) 9850 7470
Fax: +61 (2) 9850 7480
Year founded: 1964
Ownership: Nonprofit
Accreditation: Non-U.S. equivalent
Cost: $$
Special fields: Applied linguistics, early
childhood education

Offers a research-based Ph.D. in early childhood education. Residency is negotiable, and the program usually takes three to six years to complete. A Doctor of Applied Linguistics is also under development.

*"We've got the two-headed pit bull!
We've got the world's tallest mime!
We've got a 100% online regionally
accredited Ed.D. program!"*

MARYVALE INSTITUTE

Maryvale House, Old Oscott Hill
Kingstanding
Birmingham B44 9AG
United Kingdom
Web site: www.maryvale.ac.uk
Phone: +44 (121) 360 8118
Accreditation: Non-U.S. equivalent
Ownership: Nonprofit, church
Cost: $$$
Special fields: Roman Catholic religious
education

Offers a research-based D.Phil. in Catholic studies with emphasis in religious education, in association with the Pontifical University in Ireland. Residency is negotiated on a case-by-case basis, but students are generally expected to at least visit the campus for an oral defense of the dissertation.

OPEN UNIVERSITY

Walton Hall
Milton Keynes, MK7 6AA
United Kingdom
Web site: www.open.ac.uk
Email: ces-gen@open.ac.uk
Phone: +44 (1908) 274 066
Fax: +44 (1908) 653 744
Year founded: 1969
Ownership: Nonprofit
Accreditation: Non-U.S. equivalent
Cost: $$
Special fields: Child development, curriculum
& assessment, developing lifelong learning,

education/training/future of work, educational management, gender issues in education, inclusive & special education, language & literacy, primary education, teacher education & mentoring

The Open University offers an Ed.D. entirely by distance learning in the fields listed above; students initially complete a battery of coursework in the chosen field, then proceed to a dissertation. New specialization tracks may become available in 2003.

SOUTH BANK UNIVERSITY

103 Borough Road
London SE1 0AA
United Kingdom
Web site: www.southbank-university.ac.uk
Email: internat@sbu.ac.uk
Phone: +44 (20) 7815 6137
Fax: +44 (20) 7815 6199
Year founded: 1892
Ownership: Nonprofit
Accreditation: Non-U.S. equivalent
Cost: $$$

Students worldwide may apply to South Bank's research-based Ph.D. program in education. Although most students are expected to spend six weeks on campus per year, the school may be willing to negotiate with students who are unable to meet this requirement. Experienced educators with an impressive publication record may be eligible to apply to South Bank's Ph.D.-by-publication program, provided that they have a "significant connection with the University."

UNIVERSITY OF BIRMINGHAM

Edgbaston
Birmingham B15 2TT
United Kingdom
Web site: www.edu.bham.ac.uk/CPD
Email: d.eaton@bham.ac.uk
Phone: +44 (12) 1414 4856
Year founded: 1900
Ownership: Nonprofit
Accreditation: Non-U.S. equivalent
Residency: None
Cost: $$$
Special fields: Special education

Offers a research-based Ph.D. in special education (emphasis on autism, emotional behavior difficulties, learning difficulties, sensory impairment, or speech and language difficulties). Students without a strong research background are encouraged to take Birmingham's course on research training, which can be completed by correspondence.

UNIVERSITY OF BRADFORD

Student Registry, Postgraduate
Richmond Road
Bradford BD7 1DP
United Kingdom
Web site: www.brad.ac.uk
Email: pg-admissions@bradford.ac.uk
Phone: +44 (1274) 233 042
Fax: +44 (1274) 235 810
Year founded: 1957
Ownership: Nonprofit
Accreditation: Non-U.S. equivalent
Residency: Two weeks per year
Cost: $$$

Offers a research-based Ph.D. in education, with two weeks of on-campus residency per year. Likely duration: three to six years. Students must initially register for the M.Phil. before progressing to the Ph.D. program.

UNIVERSITY OF KENT AT CANTERBURY

The Registry
Canterbury, Kent CT2 7NZ
United Kingdom
Web site: www.ukc.ac.uk
Email: graduate-office@ukc.ac.uk
Phone: +44 (12) 2782 4040
Fax: +44 (12) 2745 2196
Year founded: 1965
Ownership: Nonprofit
Accreditation: Non-U.S. equivalent
Residency: Negotiable
Cost: $$$
Special fields: Applied linguistics

Offers a research-based Ph.D. in applied linguistics. Students work through an approved local facility and visit Kent for yearly residencies of negotiable duration. The program takes four to six years to complete.

UNIVERSITY OF MANCHESTER

The Research and Graduate School
Faculty of Education
Manchester M13 9PL
United Kingdom
Web site: www.man.ac.uk
Email: p.warburton@man.ac.uk
Phone: +44 (16) 1275 7891
Fax: +44 (16) 1275 7894
Year founded: 1851
Ownership: Nonprofit
Accreditation: Non-U.S. equivalent
Residency: Negotiable
Cost: $$$

Student profile: Brent Muirhead

Brent Muirhead has conducted research across a multitude of disciplines while earning three master's degrees and two doctoral degrees. He has worked as a campus minister and high school history teacher. He now teaches graduate online research classes for the University of Phoenix (UOP) and helps train and mentor their new faculty members.

Best Education Degrees: Why did you choose Capella University for your doctorate in education?

Brent Muirhead: My selection of a school was based on six basic factors: regional accreditation in the United States, adequate learner support staff, course titles that would be easily recognized by educators and business personnel, financial costs that were realistic for an educator, program flexibility, and a learner-centered philosophy.

BED: Please describe your learning experience.

BM: I enjoyed my online classes. The academic dialogue was often better than my traditional graduate classes. Professors asked thought-provoking questions that were intellectually challenging and created lively online interaction with a diverse student population. The teachers provided expertise that helped make my dissertation to be on the cutting edge of distance education.

BED: Would you recommend this particular program to others? Why?

BM: I would recommend the Ph.D. degree in education at Capella University because they truly offer a relevant and student-centered education. Students are given the freedom to develop papers and projects that fit their professional goals.

BED: Would you recommend distance learning in general to others?

BM: The online process helps students gain practical writing experiences. Students learn to translate their ideas into narratives that effectively communicate across cultures. Writing is a powerful tool that offers numerous opportunities for students to display their depth of knowledge, organizational skills, reflective insights, and the ability to explore new ideas. Today's employers are looking for people who can effectively communicate in our global community.

BED: In your opinion, what type of person makes a good distance-learning student?

BM: My personal experience and research studies have identified four primary competencies that are essential for online students: computer skills (word processing and email), literacy and discussion skills, time management skills, and interactive skills. Distance education literature reveals a strong emphasis on students who are motivated and are self-reliant.

BED: How did earning this degree enhance your career?

BM: My Ph.D. degree in education has helped me move from being a high school teacher to a graduate educator at the University of Phoenix. I am an expert in interactivity (communication, participation, and feedback) in distance education schools. I have been published in several journals such as *Educational Technology & Society*, an electronic journal that reaches readers in 110 countries. I have been published over 50 times and my letters have appeared frequently in *USA Today*, *The New York Times*, and *Atlanta Journal* newspapers. It is exciting to have Walter Cronkite's and Gail Sheehy's letters follow mine!

Offers a Ph.D. in education by research. On a case-by-case basis, it may be possible to arrange to undertake such a program in a low-residency format.

UNIVERSITY OF MELBOURNE

Victoria, 3010
Australia
Web site: www.unimelb.edu.au/research
Email: j.gilbert@sgs.unimelb.edu.au
Phone: +61 (3) 8344 8670
Year founded: 1853
Ownership: Nonprofit
Accreditation: Non-U.S. equivalent
Cost: $$
Special fields: Applied linguistics, computer-assisted language learning, computer education, education (general), English as a second language, health & physical education, mathematics education

One of the most prestigious research universities in Australia, Melbourne makes its research Ph.D. programs available to students worldwide who are able to find, and work through, an approved local institution (the list of approved institutions is already fairly extensive, and students may petition to have new institutions added to the list). The program involves four to six years of study and a dissertation of about 100,000 words.

UNIVERSITY OF NEW ENGLAND

School of Education Studies
Armidale, New South Wales 2351
Australia
Web site: www.une.edu.au
Email: ipo@metz.une.edu.au
Phone: +61 (2) 6773 3872
Fax: +61 (2) 6773 3350
Year founded: 1938
Ownership: Nonprofit
Accreditation: Non-U.S. equivalent
Cost: $$
Special fields: Curriculum studies, education studies, special education

Offers Ph.D. and Ed.D. programs in curriculum studies, education studies, and special education through off-campus study (though some campus visits may be required). The Ph.D. is generally research-based, while the Ed.D. requires some preliminary doctoral coursework. Either can be completed in four to six years. UNE is the oldest distance education provider in Australia.

UNIVERSITY OF SOUTH AFRICA

P.O. Box 392
Unisa 0003
South Africa
Web site: www.unisa.ac.za
Email: study-info@alpha.unisa.ac.za
Phone: +27 (12) 429 3111
Fax: +27 (12) 429 3221
Year founded: 1873
Ownership: Nonprofit, state
Accreditation: Non-U.S. equivalent
Cost: $
Special fields: Comparative education, education management, history of education, philosophy of education, psychology of education, socio-education, special needs education

Offers a research-based Ed.D. in any of the fields listed above. The dissertation runs to 60,000–80,000 words, and the program takes an average three to five years to complete. No residency is required. UNISA has recently begun to more aggressively seek U.S. students, and a correspondent tells us that UNISA may also be seeking additional accreditation through the Distance Education and Training Council (DETC).

UNIVERSITY OF SOUTH AUSTRALIA

GPO Box 2471
Adelaide, South Australia 5001
Australia
Web site: www.unisa.edu.au
Email: international.office@unisa.edu.au
Phone: +61 (8) 8302 0114
Fax: +61 (8) 8302 0233
Year founded: 1991
Ownership: Nonprofit
Accreditation: Non-U.S. equivalent
Cost: $$
Special fields: Early childhood education, education

Offers an Ed.D. (general or in early childhood education) through a mix of online and/or correspondence-based coursework and research, and an entirely research-based Ph.D. in education. Either program can be completed in three to six years.

UNIVERSITY OF SOUTHERN QUEENSLAND

International Office
Toowoomba, Queensland 4350
Australia
Web site: www.usq.edu.au
Email: international@usq.edu.au
Phone: +61 (74) 631 2362
Fax: +61 (74) 636 2211

Student profile: Cindy Knott

Dr. Cindy Knott has been in the education field for over 20 years. The majority of her experience has been teaching in the public school system, primarily at the special education junior high level. She has also been an assistant director at a private setting for severely emotionally behavior-disturbed children. Her current position is Education Campus College Chair at University of Phoenix Online. She received her Doctor of Education (Ed.D.) from Nova Southeastern University.

Best Education Degrees: Why did you choose the institution that you did?

Cindy Knott: Nova Southeastern University provided the degree that I wanted to pursue, while still being able to work. Its pragmatic content was useful in my teaching setting. It is an accredited institution with a solid program. Nova allowed the completion of the degree and making a difference in what you do all at the same time.

BED: Please describe your learning experience.

CK: The learning experience was a very positive experience as a whole. Each course built on each other and the dissertation coursework was integrated into the program throughout the three years, unlike traditional universities. The research project focused on school improvement and student achievement, making an impact on your setting. Generally, the professors were current in the field and very knowledgeable about the course content. Summer institutes were mandatory for two out of the three years. Doctoral candidates in the Ed.D. program from all over the nation attended. This was a unique opportunity to meet and network with other professionals.

BED: Would you recommend this particular program to others? Why?

CK: I would recommend this particular program to others for the flexibility in the program, application of skills and knowledge, and quality level of instruction. Doctoral students are able to participate in the program while working. The advantage is the practicality of learned skills throughout the program. You are able to apply what you learn immediately to your work environment.

BED: How did earning this degree enhance your career?

CK: Earning my doctorate degree enhanced my goal to work in higher education and distance education. It enabled me to meet my professional goals and make a career move from teaching in the K–12 setting to facilitating in an online higher education environment.

It is important that you keep the rain off your lessons en route to the post office.

Year founded: 1967
Ownership: Nonprofit
Accreditation: Non-U.S. equivalent
Cost: $$
Special fields: Professional leadership

Applicants to the Ed.D. program in professional leadership must have at least three years of experience as an educator or administrator. The program takes five to eight years to complete, but can apparently be done entirely off-campus. Students complete six research courses (which can be done by correspondence, and may be available online soon) and a dissertation. Specialization tracks are available in leadership/management/policy analysis, pedagogy, and special education/guidance counseling.

UNIVERSITY OF TASMANIA

Board of Graduate Studies by Research
Churchill Avenue, Sandy Bay
G.P.O. Box 252-45
Hobart, Tasmania 7001
Australia
Web site: www.international.utas.edu.au
Email: international.office@utas.edu.au
Phone: +61 (3) 6226 2762
Fax: +61 (3) 6226 7497
Year founded: 1890
Ownership: Nonprofit
Accreditation: Non-U.S. equivalent
Cost: $$

Offers a Ph.D. in education by research (four to six years of study culminating in a dissertation of about 100,000 words) or on the basis of prior work (be it published or unpublished). Students who opt for the latter option must write a comprehensive guide to the prior work, explaining how it constitutes a doctoral-level contribution to the field of education.

UNIVERSITY OF TECHNOLOGY, SYDNEY

P.O. Box 123
Broadway, New South Wales 2007
Australia
Web site: www.gradschool.uts.edu.au
Email: info.office@uts.edu.au
Phone: +61 (2) 9514 2000
Year founded: 1965
Ownership: Nonprofit
Accreditation: Non-U.S. equivalent
Cost: $$
Special fields: Adult & vocational education,
   teacher education

Offers a Ph.D. by publication in adult and vocational education or teacher education to established researchers, based on their record of academic publication and original scholarly contribution to knowledge. An applicant must submit all of his/her relevant work and an integrative paper explaining the work.

UNIVERSITY OF WALES—ABERYSTWYTH

Old College, King Street
Aberystwyth, Ceredigion
Wales SY23 2AX
United Kingdom
Web site: www.aber.ac.uk
Email: rlw@aber.ac.uk
Phone: +44 (1970) 622 090
Fax: +44 (1970) 622 921
Year founded: 1872
Ownership: Nonprofit
Accreditation: Non-U.S. equivalent
Cost: $$$

Offers a Ph.D. in education by research. Students may work on the program part-time (traveling to Wales for yearly campus visits, generally of two to three weeks duration), or research full-time through a place of employment.

In this symbolic demonstration, Ludmilla represents pedagogy, while Sergei dances the role of andragogy.

Other possibilities for research doctorates

Research doctorates are almost never advertised as distance-learning programs and, since residency is generally negotiated on a case-by-case basis, this means that there are very likely *many* low-residency research doctorate opportunities that have slipped our notice.

Here are the names and addresses of a few additional universities where readers have told us that they are doing nonresident or very-low-residency research doctorates. If you're successful in articulating a research arrangement with one of them, we would love to hear about it; please feel free to email us at *bed@degree.net.*

The United Kingdom

ASTON UNIVERSITY
Aston Triangle, Birmingham B4 7ET, England
www.aston.ac.uk

COVENTRY UNIVERSITY
Priory Street, Coventry CV1 5FB, England
www.coventry.ac.uk

DE MONTFORT UNIVERSITY
The Gateway, Leicester LE1 9BH, England
www.dmu.ac.uk

HERIOT-WATT UNIVERSITY
Edinburgh EH14 4AS, Scotland
www.hw.ac.uk

KEELE UNIVERSITY
Keele, Staffordshire ST5 5BG, England
www.keele.ac.uk

MANCHESTER METROPOLITAN UNIVERSITY
All Saints, Manchester M15 6BH, England
www.mmu.ac.uk

OXFORD BROOKES UNIVERSITY
Gipsy Lane, Headington, Oxford OX3 0BP, England
www.brookes.ac.uk

THAMES VALLEY UNIVERSITY
St. Mary's Road, Ealing, London W5 5RF, England
www.tvu.ac.uk

UNIVERSITY OF ABERDEEN
King's College, Aberdeen AB24 3FX, Scotland
www.abdn.ac.uk

UNIVERSITY OF BRIGHTON
Mithras House, Brighton BN2 4AT, England
www.bton.ac.uk

UNIVERSITY OF DUNDEE
Nethergate, Dundee DD1 4HN, Scotland
www.dundee.ac.uk

UNIVERSITY OF DURHAM
Old Shire Hall, Durham DH1 3HP, England
www.dur.ac.uk

UNIVERSITY OF EDINBURGH
South Bridge, Edinburgh EH8 9YL, Scotland
www.ed.ac.uk

UNIVERSITY OF GLASGOW
Glasgow, G12 8QQ, Scotland
www.gla.ac.uk

UNIVERSITY OF KENT AT CANTERBURY
Canterbury, Kent CT2 7NZ, England
www.ukc.ac.uk

UNIVERSITY OF LONDON
Senate House, Malet Street, London WC1E 7HU, England
www.lon.ac.uk

UNIVERSITY OF LUTON
Park Square, Luton LU1 3JU, England
www.luton.ac.uk

UNIVERSITY OF NEWCASTLE-UPON-TYNE
Newcastle-upon-Tyne, NE1 7RU, England
www.ncl.ac.uk

UNIVERSITY OF NORTHUMBRIA AT NEWCASTLE
Ellison Place, Newcastle-upon-Tyne NE1 8ST, England
www.unn.ac.uk

UNIVERSITY OF SHEFFIELD
Western Bank, Sheffield S10 2TN, England
www.shef.ac.uk

UNIVERSITY OF STIRLING
Stirling, FK9 4LA, Scotland
www.stir.ac.uk

UNIVERSITY OF STRATHCLYDE
16 Richmond Street, Glasgow G1 1XQ, Scotland
www.strath.ac.uk

UNIVERSITY OF WALES—BANGOR
Bangor, Gwynedd LL57 2DG, Wales
www.bangor.ac.uk

UNIVERSITY OF WALES—CARDIFF
50 Park Place, Cardiff CF10 3UA, Wales
www.cf.ac.uk

UNIVERSITY OF WALES—LAMPETER
Ceredigion, SA48 7ED, Wales
www.lamp.ac.uk

UNIVERSITY OF WARWICK
Coventry, CV4 7AL, England
www.warwick.ac.uk

UNIVERSITY OF THE WEST OF ENGLAND
Coldharbour Lane, Bristol BS16 1QY, England
www.uwe.ac.uk

UNIVERSITY OF WESTMINSTER
309 Regent Street, London W1R 8AL, England
www.westminster.ac.uk

Australia

CENTRAL QUEENSLAND UNIVERSITY
Bruce Highway, Rockhampton, Queensland 4702
www.cqu.edu.au

CHARLES STURT UNIVERSITY
Panorama Avenue, Bathurst, New South Wales 2795
www.csu.edu.au

CURTIN UNIVERSITY OF TECHNOLOGY
G.P.O. Box U 1987, Perth, Western Australia 6845
www.curtin.edu.au

DEAKIN UNIVERSITY
221 Burwood Highway, Burwood, Victoria 3125
www.deakin.edu.au

South Africa

POTCHEFSTROOM UNIVERSITY FOR CHRISTIAN HIGHER EDUCATION
Private Bag X6001, Potchefstroom 2520
www.puk.ac.za

UNIVERSITY OF PRETORIA
Pretoria 0002
www.up.ac.za

VISTA UNIVERSITY
Private Bag X634, Pretoria 0001
www.vista.ac.za

India

CENTRAL INSTITUTE OF ENGLISH AND FOREIGN LANGUAGES
Hyderabad 500 007, Andra Pradesh

Japan

RIKKYO UNIVERSITY
3-34-1 Nishi-Ikebukuro, Toshima-ku, Tokyo 171-8501
www.rikkyo.ac.jp

Pakistan

ALLAMA IQBAL OPEN UNIVERSITY
Sector H-8, Islamabad
www.aiou.edu.pk

State Offices for Teacher Licensure

To teach public school in the United States, you need a teaching license (often referred to as a credential or certificate). As these licenses are issued and regulated at the state level, what is required to obtain a license can vary widely from one state to the next. To find out the criteria for your state, consult the government office in your state that handles teacher licensure. Below you will find contact information for all 50 teacher licensing offices in the United States. Almost all of them post their requirements on their Web sites. For more information on the credentialing process, see chapter 3.

ALABAMA STATE DEPARTMENT OF EDUCATION
Office of Teacher Education and Certification
P.O. Box 302101
Montgomery, AL 36130-2101
Phone: (334) 242 9977
Web site: www.alsde.edu/ver1/
section_detail.asp?section=66
Email: tcert@alsde.edu

**ALASKA DEPARTMENT OF EDUCATION
AND EARLY DEVELOPMENT**
Office of Teacher Education and Certification
Goldbelt Building
801 W. 10th Street, Ste. 200
Juneau, AK 99801-1894
Phone: (907) 465 2831
Fax: (907) 465 244
Web site: www.eed.state.ak.us/
TeacherCertification
Email: certify@eed.state.ak.us

ARIZONA DEPARTMENT OF EDUCATION
Teacher Certification Unit
P.O. Box 6490
Phoenix, AZ 85005
Phone: (602) 542 4367
Fax: (602) 542 1141

Web site: www.ade.state.az.us/prodev/
certification
Email: certification@mail1.ade.state.az.us

ARKANSAS DEPARTMENT OF EDUCATION
Office of Professional Licensure
Room 109B, 4 Capitol Mall
Little Rock, AR 72201
Phone: (501) 682 4344
Web site: arkedu.state.ar.us/teacher.htm

**CALIFORNIA COMMISSION ON
TEACHER CREDENTIALING**
Professional Services Division
1900 Capitol Avenue
Sacramento, CA 95814-7000
Phone: (916) 445 0184 • (888) 921 2682
Web site:
www.ctc.ca.gov/credentialinfo/credinfo.html
Email: credentials@ctc.ca.gov

COLORADO DEPARTMENT OF EDUCATION
Office of Professional Services
Educator Licensing
201 East Colfax Avenue, Room 105
Denver, CO 80203
Phone: (303) 866 6628
Fax: (303) 866 6866
Web site: www.cde.state.co.us/index_license.htm

CONNECTICUT STATE DEPARTMENT OF EDUCATION

Bureau of Certification and Professional
Development
P.O. Box 150471 - Room 243
Hartford, Connecticut 06115-0471
Phone: (860) 566 5201
Fax: (860) 566 8929
Web site:
www.state.ct.us/sde/dtl/cert/index.htm
Email: teacher.cert@po.state.ct.us

STATE OF DELAWARE

Department of Education
Office of Certification
John G. Townsend Building
P.O. Box 1402
Dover, DE 19903-1402
Phone: (888) 759 9133
Web site: deeds.doe.state.de.us/crt/
deeds_crt_default.asp

DISTRICT OF COLUMBIA PUBLIC SCHOOLS

Teacher Education and Certification Branch
825 North Capitol Street, N.E.
Washington, DC 20002-4232
Phone: (202) 442 5377
Web site: www.k12.dc.us/dcps/home.html

FLORIDA DEPARTMENT OF EDUCATION

Bureau of Educator Certification
Suite 201, Turlington Building
325 West Gaines Street
Tallahassee, Florida 32399-0400
Phone: (850) 488 5724 • (800) 445 6739
Web site: www.firn.edu/doe/bin00022/
home0022.htm
Email: edcert@mail.doe.state.fl.us

GEORGIA PROFESSIONAL STANDARDS COMMISSION

Office of Teacher Education and Certification
1454 Twin Towers East
Atlanta, GA 30334
Phone: (404) 657 9000
Web site:
www.gapsc.com/TeacherCertification.asp

HAWAI'I DEPARTMENT OF EDUCATION

P.O. Box 2360
Honolulu, Hawai'i 96804
Phone: (808) 586 3230
Fax: (808) 586 3234
Web site: www.k12.hi.us/~personnl/license.html

IDAHO STATE DEPARTMENT OF EDUCATION

Teacher Certification
P.O. Box 83720
Boise, ID 83720-0027
Phone: (208) 332 6884
Web site: www.sde.state.id.us/certification
Email: kpotter@sde.state.id.us

ILLINOIS STATE BOARD OF EDUCATION

Office of Teacher Education and Certification
100 North First Street
Springfield, IL 62777-0001
Phone: (800) 845 8749
Fax: (217) 524 1289
Web site: www.isbe.state.il.us/teachers.htm

INDIANA PROFESSIONAL STANDARDS BOARD

Office of Teacher Education and Certification
Two Market Square Center
251 East Ohio Street, Suite 201
Indianapolis, IN 46204-2133
Phone: (317) 232 9010
Fax: (317) 232 9023
Web site: www.state.in.us/psb
Email: helpdesk@psb.state.in.us

IOWA DEPARTMENT OF EDUCATION

Board of Educational Examiners
Grimes State Office Building
E. 14th & Grand
Des Moines, IA 50319
Phone: (515) 281 5294
Fax: (515) 242 5988
Web site: www.state.ia.us/educate/programs/
boee/require.html
Email: christina.dykstra@ed.state.ia.us

KANSAS STATE BOARD OF EDUCATION

Office of Teacher Certification
120 S.E. 10th Avenue
Topeka, KS 66612-1182
Phone: (785) 296 8010
Fax: (785) 296 4318
Web site: www.ksbe.state.ks.us/cert/cert.html
Email: mgage@ksde.org

KENTUCKY DEPARTMENT OF EDUCATION

Education Professional Standards Board
Division of Certification
1024 Capital Center Drive
Frankfort, KY 40601
Phone: (502) 564 4606
Web site: www.kde.state.ky.us/otec/cert
Email: jbanta@kde.state.ky.us

Mr. Illingworth discovers research doctorates.

LOUISIANA STATE DEPARTMENT OF EDUCATION
Division of Teacher Standards, Assessment, and
    Certification
P.O. Box 94064
Baton Rouge, LA 70804-9064
Phone: (225) 342 3490
Fax: (225) 342 3499
Web site: www.doe.state.la.us/DOE/asps/
    home.asp?I=DTSAC
Email: stalamo@mail.doe.state.la.us

MAINE DEPARTMENT OF EDUCATION
Certification Office
23 State House Station
Augusta, ME 04333
Phone: (207) 287 5315
Web site: www.state.me.us/education/cert/
    cert.htm
Email: pat.julien@state.me.us

MARYLAND STATE DEPARTMENT OF EDUCATION
Division of Certification and Accreditation
200 W. Baltimore Street
Baltimore, MD 21201-2595
Phone: (410) 767 0412
Web site: www.msde.state.md.us/certification/
    index.htm

MASSACHUSETTS DEPARTMENT OF EDUCATION
Office of Certification and Credentialing
350 Main Street
Malden, MA 02148-5023
Phone: (781) 338 3000 ext. 6600
Fax: (781) 338 3391
Web site: www.doe.mass.edu/cert
Email: cert.inquiries@doe.mass.edu

MICHIGAN DEPARTMENT OF EDUCATION
Office of Professional Preparation Services
608 West Allegan
Lansing, MI 48933
Phone: (517) 373 3310
Web site: www.state.mi.us/mde/off/ppc
Email: jenkinsf@state.mi.us

MINNESOTA BOARD OF TEACHING
Office of Teacher Education and Certification
1500 Highway 36 West
Roseville, MN 55113-4266
Phone: (651) 582 8833
Fax: (651) 582 8872
Web site: cfl.state.mn.us/licen/license.htm
Email: board.teaching@state.mn.us

MISSISSIPPI STATE DEPARTMENT OF EDUCATION
Office of Educator Licensure
Central High School Building
P.O. Box 771
Jackson, MS 39205-0771
Phone: (601) 359 3483
Web site: www.mde.k12.ms.us/license
Email: cchester@mde.k12.ms.us

**MISSOURI DEPARTMENT OF ELEMENTARY
AND SECONDARY EDUCATION**
Division of Teacher Quality and Urban Education
Teacher Certification
P.O. Box 480
Jefferson City, MO 65102-0480
Phone: (573) 751 0051
Fax: (573) 526 3580
Web site: services.dese.state.mo.us/
    divurbteached/teachcert

MONTANA OFFICE OF PUBLIC INSTRUCTION
Certification and Licensure
Box 202501
Helena, MT 59620-2501
Phone: (406) 444 3150
Web site: www.metnet.state.mt.us/Cert/HTM
Email: cert@state.mt.us

NEBRASKA DEPARTMENT OF EDUCATION
Office of Teacher Education and Certification
301 Centennial Mall South

It takes this many people to ascertain the meaning of special education laws.

P.O. Box 94987
Lincoln, NE 68509-4987
Phone: (402) 471 2496
Web site: www.nde.state.ne.us/TCERT/
    TCERT.html
Email: tcertweb@nde4.nde.state.ne.us

NEVADA DEPARTMENT OF EDUCATION
Teacher Licensure
1820 E. Sahara, Ste. 205
Las Vegas, NV 89104-3746
Phone: (702) 486 6458
Web site: www.nde.state.nv.us/licensure/
    index.html
Email: license@nsn.k12.nv.us

NEW HAMPSHIRE DEPARTMENT OF EDUCATION
Bureau of Credentialing
101 Pleasant Street
Concord, NH 03301
Phone: (603) 271 2407
Web site: www.ed.state.nh.us/Certification/
    teacher.htm
Email: jfillion@ed.state.nh.us

NEW JERSEY DEPARTMENT OF EDUCATION
Office of Licensing and Credentials
240 West State Street
Trenton, NJ 08625-1216
Phone: (609) 292 2045
Web site: www.state.nj.us/njded/educators/
    license/index.html

NEW MEXICO STATE DEPARTMENT OF EDUCATION
Professional Licensure Unit
Education Building
300 Don Gaspar Street
Santa Fe, NM 87501-2786
Phone: (505) 827 6587
Fax: (505) 827 4148
Web site: sde.state.nm.us/divisions/ais/
    licensure/index.html
Email: emartinez@sde.state.nm.us

NEW YORK STATE EDUCATION DEPARTMENT
Office of Teaching
Room 5 North, Education Building
89 Washington Avenue
Albany, NY 12234
Phone: (518) 474 3901
Web site: www.highered.nysed.gov/tcert
Email: tcert@mail.nysed.gov

NORTH CAROLINA DEPARTMENT OF PUBLIC INSTRUCTION
Licensure Section
301 North Wilmington Street
Raleigh, NC 27601-2825
Phone: (919) 807 3310 • (800) 577 7994
Web site: www.ncpublicschools.org/licensure
Email: licensure@dpi.state.nc.us

NORTH DAKOTA EDUCATION STANDARDS AND PRACTICES BOARD
Office of Teacher Certification
State Capitol, 9th Floor
Department 202
600 East Boulevard Avenue
Bismarck, ND 58505-0440
Phone: (701) 328 2264
Fax: (701) 328 2215
Web site: www.state.nd.us/espb/
    licensure/licen.htm
Email: bthompso@state.nd.us

OHIO DEPARTMENT OF EDUCATION
Office of Certification/Licensure
65 South Front Street, Room 1009

Columbus, OH 43215-4183
Phone: (614) 466 3593
Web site: www.ode.state.oh.us/tp/ctp/candl.htm

OKLAHOMA COMMISSION FOR TEACHER PREPARATION

Office of Teacher Education and Certification
4545 N. Lincoln Blvd., Ste. 275
Oklahoma City, OK 73105-3418
Phone: (405) 525 2612
Fax: (405) 525 0373
Web site: www.octp.org
Email: octp@octp.org

OREGON TEACHER STANDARDS AND PRACTICES COMMISSION

Office of Teacher Education and Certification
255 Capitol Street, NE, Ste. 105
Salem, OR 97310-1332
Phone: (503) 378 3586
Fax: (503) 378 4448
Web site: www.tspc.state.or.us
Email: contact.tspc@state.or.us

PUERTO RICO DEPARTMENT OF EDUCATION

Office of Teacher Education and Certification
P.O. Box 190759
San Juan, PR 00919-0759
Phone: (809) 759 2000
Web site: www.de.gobierno.pr

PENNSYLVANIA DEPARTMENT OF EDUCATION

Bureau of Teacher Certification and Preparation
333 Market Street
Harrisburg, PA 17126-0333
Phone: (717) 787 3356
Web site: www.pde.psu.edu/certification/
teachcert.html

RHODE ISLAND DEPARTMENT OF ELEMENTARY AND SECONDARY EDUCATION

Office of Teacher Preparation and Certification
Shepard Building
255 Westminster Street
Providence, RI 02903
Phone: (401) 222 4600
Web site: www.ridoe.net/teacher_cert
Email: biofem@ride.ri.net

SOUTH CAROLINA DEPARTMENT OF EDUCATION

Division of Teacher Quality
Office of Teacher Certification
1600 Gervais Street
Columbia, SC 29201

Phone: (803) 734 8466 • (877) 885 5280
Fax: (803) 734 2873
Web site: www.scteachers.org/scteachers/
Cert/Certification.htm
Email: certification@scteachers.org

SOUTH DAKOTA DEPARTMENT OF EDUCATIONAL AND CULTURAL AFFAIRS

Office of Policy and Accountability
700 Governors Drive
Pierre, SD 57501
Phone: (605) 773 3553
Fax: (605) 773 6139
Web site: www.state.sd.us/deca/account/
certif.htm
Email: gwen.rothenberger@state.sd.us

TENNESSEE DEPARTMENT OF EDUCATION

Office of Teacher Licensing
5th Floor, Andrew Johnson Tower
710 James Robertson Parkway
Nashville, TN 37243-0375
Phone: (615) 532 4885
Web site:
www.state.tn.us/education/lic_home.htm
Email: phobbins@mail.state.tn.us

TEXAS STATE BOARD FOR EDUCATOR CERTIFICATION

1001 Trinity
Austin, TX 78701
Phone: (512) 469 3000 • (888) 863 5880
Fax: (512) 469 3018
Web site: www.sbec.state.tx.us
Email: sbec@mail.sbec.state.tx.us

UTAH STATE OFFICE OF EDUCATION

Certification and Personnel Development
250 East 500 South
Salt Lake City, UT 84111
Phone: (801) 538 7740
Fax: (801) 538 7973
Web site: www.usoe.k12.ut.us/cert
Email: jbrown@usoe.k12.ut.us

VERMONT DEPARTMENT OF EDUCATION

Licensing Office
120 State Street
Montpelier, VT 05620-2501
Phone: (802) 828 2445
Web site: www.state.vt.us/educ/license/
index.htm
Email: licensing@doe.state.vt.us

VIRGINIA DEPARTMENT OF EDUCATION

Office of Teacher Education and Certification
P.O. Box 2120
Richmond, VA 23216-2120
Phone: (804) 371 2522
Web site: www.pen.k12.va.us/VDOE/
newvdoe/teached.html

WASHINGTON STATE DEPARTMENT OF PUBLIC INSTRUCTION

Professional Education and Certification
Old Capitol Building
P.O. Box 47200
Olympia, WA 98504-7200
Phone: (360) 753 6773
Fax: (360) 586 0145
Web site: www.k12.wa.us/cert
Email: cert@ospi.wednet.edu

WEST VIRGINIA DEPARTMENT OF EDUCATION

Office of Teacher Education and Certification
1900 Kanawha Blvd. East
Bldg. #6, Room B-252
Charleston, WV 25305-0330
Phone: (800) 982 2378
Web site: wvde.state.wv.us/certification
Email: mbowe@access.k12.wv.us

WISCONSIN DEPARTMENT OF PUBLIC INSTRUCTION

Bureau for Teacher Education and Licensing Teams
125 South Webster Street, P.O. Box 7841
Madison, WI 53707-7841
Phone: (800) 266 1027
Fax: (608) 264 9558
Web site: www.dpi.state.wi.us/dpi/dlsis/tel
Email: tcert@dpi.state.wi.us

WYOMING PROFESSIONAL TEACHING STANDARDS BOARD

Office of Teacher Education and Certification
2300 Capitol Avenue, Hathaway 2nd Floor
Cheyenne, WY 82002
Phone: (307) 777 7291 • (800) 675 6893
Fax: (307) 777 6234
Web site: www.k12.wy.us/ptsb/index.html
Email: ptsb@www.k12.wy.us

For More Information on Schools in This Book

If you have questions about one of the schools described in this book, don't hesitate to write to us. We'll do our best to help. These are the ground rules:

What to do before writing to us

▶ Point your Web browser to *www.degree.net/updates/bed*. At this Web site we will post updates and corrections to the school listings in this book.

▶ Do your own homework. Check with your local library, the relevant state education department, or the Better Business Bureau first, as well as, of course, the Internet.

▶ Schools do move, and the post office will only forward mail for a short while. If a letter comes back as "undeliverable," call directory assistance ("information") in the school's city and see if a number is listed. They can give you a new street address as well.

▶ Schools do change phone numbers, and the telephone company will only notify you of the new number for a short while. If you can't reach a school by phone, write to it, or try directory assistance to see if there has been a change.

Writing to us

If you cannot reach a school by phone or mail, if you have information you would like to share, or if you have any questions or problems, then please write and let us know. We may be able to help.

▶ Enclose a self-addressed, stamped envelope. If you are outside the United States, enclose two international postal reply coupons, available at your post office.

▶ If you want extensive advice or opinions on your personal situation, you will need to use the Degree Consulting Service that John

In the midst of applying to a Ph.D. program, Jean-Paul Sartre realizes that his middle initial does not exist.

established (though he no longer runs it). This service is described in Appendix D.

▶ Don't get too annoyed if we don't respond promptly. We do our best, but we get overwhelmed sometimes and we travel a lot.

▶ Please don't telephone.

▶ *Write to us at:*
Best Education Degrees
Degree.net
P.O. Box 7123
Berkeley, CA 94707   USA

▶ *Or email us at* *bed@degree.net.*

Do let us know of any mistakes or outdated information you find in this book; we will post corrections at *www.degree.net/updates/bed.*

All About Accreditation (and How to Check If a School Has Got It)

Let us begin by saying that if you stick to the schools listed in this book, accreditation is not something you need to worry about: All of the schools discussed here are legitimately accredited and their degrees universally accepted in the world of education. But for those who want to know more about this complex topic—perhaps you're looking into a school not listed in this book and want to know if it's legit—here's a brief overview of accreditation and why it's so important, especially for someone embarked on a teaching career.

What Is Accreditation?

Would you buy a degree from this man?

Quite simply, it is a validation—a statement by a group of persons who are, theoretically, impartial experts in higher education, that a given school, or department within a school, has been thoroughly investigated and found worthy of approval.

Accreditation is a peculiarly American concept. In every other country in the world, all colleges and universities are either operated by the government, or given the right to grant degrees directly by the government, so there is no need for an independent agency to say that a given school is OK.

In the U.S., on the other hand, a school doesn't need government approval to open and operate, at least not on the federal level. (Some individual states require that a degree-granting school have, or be working toward, recognized accreditation.) Accreditation, therefore, is a voluntary process, done by private, nongovernmental agencies.

As a result of this lack of central control or authority, there have evolved hundreds of accrediting agencies: good and bad, recognized and unrecognized, legitimate and phony. For better or for worse, certain legitimate accrediting agencies have emerged as arbiters of what's an acceptable degree in the worlds of business and academia. Other accrediting agencies are completely bogus, creations of the schools they accredit for misleading marketing purposes.

So when a school says, "We are accredited," that statement alone means nothing. You must always ask, "Accredited by whom?"

The Accreditation Your Degree Needs

Teaching licenses, teaching jobs, graduate programs—those without a properly accredited degree need not apply. A degree that is not properly accredited is effectively treated as no degree at all. In some cases, accreditation standards are explicit: a state's teacher licensing requirements, for example, will specify a "regionally accredited bachelor's degree." In other cases, such a requirement might be de facto practice rather than written law: in the admission departments of graduate schools for example. Either way, the degree without the right kind of accreditation is unusable.

Is this fair to unaccredited schools? Not really. Lack of accreditation doesn't mean a school is bad. Remember, all schools start out unaccredited and must operate for at least a few years before they can apply for accreditation. This creates a conundrum: A school can't get accredited until it has students, and it's hard to attract students until it is accredited. You, however, cannot afford to put your teaching career on the line for someone else's catch-22. If a school is not properly accredited—no matter how exciting the curriculum, enlightened the faculty, and promising its future—we can't recommend it, because its degree won't be useful to you.

These are the types of accepted accreditation that are relevant to the world of education:

Regional accreditation

The most widely accepted form of institutional accreditation in the United States is called regional accreditation. Six agencies, all recognized by the U.S. Department of Education, are each responsible for a certain region of the country. In many cases, especially in the world of education, it is the *only* recognized form of accreditation.

MIDDLE STATES ASSOCIATION OF COLLEGES AND SCHOOLS
Commission on Higher Education
3624 Market Street
Philadelphia, PA 19104
(215) 662 5606 • Fax: (215) 662 5501 • Web site: www.msache.org
Delaware, District of Columbia, Maryland, New Jersey, New York, Pennsylvania, Puerto Rico, Virgin Islands.

NEW ENGLAND ASSOCIATION OF SCHOOLS AND COLLEGES
209 Burlington Road
Bedford, MA 01730
(781) 271 0022 • Fax: (781) 271 0950 • Web site: www.neasc.org
Connecticut, Maine, Massachusetts, New Hampshire, Rhode Island, Vermont.

NORTH CENTRAL ASSOCIATION OF COLLEGES AND SCHOOLS
30 North La Salle Street, Suite 2400
Chicago, IL 60602
(800) 621 7440 • Fax: (312) 263 7462 • Web site: www.ncacihe.org
Arizona, Arkansas, Colorado, Illinois, Indiana, Iowa, Kansas, Michigan, Minnesota, Missouri, Nebraska, New Mexico, North Dakota, Ohio, Oklahoma, South Dakota, West Virginia, Wisconsin, Wyoming.

NORTHWEST ASSOCIATION OF SCHOOLS AND COLLEGES

11300 NE 33rd Place, Suite 120

Bellevue, WA 98004

(425) 827 2005 • Fax: (425) 827 3395 • Web site: www.cocnasc.org

Alaska, Idaho, Montana, Nevada, Oregon, Utah, Washington.

SOUTHERN ASSOCIATION OF COLLEGES AND SCHOOLS

1866 Southern Lane

Decatur, GA 30033

(404) 679 4500 • Fax: (404) 679 4558 • Web site: www.sacs.org

Alabama, Florida, Georgia, Kentucky, Louisiana, Mississippi, North Carolina, South Carolina, Tennessee, Texas, Virginia.

WESTERN ASSOCIATION OF SCHOOLS AND COLLEGES

985 Atlantic Ave., Suite 100

Alameda, CA 94501

(510) 748 9001 • Fax: (510) 748 9797 • Web site: www.wascweb.org

California, Hawaii, Guam, Trust Territory of the Pacific.

How to check out a school not in this book

It's quite possible that you'll encounter an interesting-looking program not covered in this book, and want to check up on its legitimacy and acceptability. We suggest the following steps:

▶ Check *Bears' Guide to Earning Degrees by Distance Learning*, also published by Ten Speed Press, which is a complete source for all distance-learning and nontraditional degree programs. In it we list over 2,500 schools (good, bad, and otherwise) and over 150 accreditors (good, bad, and otherwise). For more information on the book and how to get a copy, visit our Web site at *www.degree.net*.

▶ If the school isn't described in *Bears' Guide*, and is located in the United States, use the contact information in this chapter to check if the school is accredited by the appropriate regional accreditor or the DETC.

▶ If the school isn't described in *Bears' Guide*, and is located in Great Britain or the British Commonwealth, we recommend checking the *Commonwealth Universities Yearbook*,

published annually and available at many university libraries.

▶ If the school isn't described in *Bears' Guide*, and is located in Australia, we suggest contacting the Australian Qualifications Framework (*www.aqf.edu.au*).

▶ If the school isn't described in *Bears' Guide*, and is located elsewhere, we recommend that prospective U.S. students contact the American Association of Collegiate Registrars and Admissions Officers (*www.aacrao.com*) for further guidance, and that prospective students in other countries contact their national Ministry of Education or equivalent agency for further guidance.

If none of the above approaches produce any useful information, then write to us and we will do what we can to help:

Best Education Degrees
Degree.net
P.O. Box 7123
Berkeley, CA 94707 USA
bed@degree.net

Distance Education and Training Council

A "silver standard" of accreditation has emerged in the form of the Distance Education and Training Council (DETC), a U.S.-based agency that deals exclusively with schools that offer most or all of their programs through distance learning. Although recognized by the U.S. Department of Education, and widely accepted in the business world, DETC accreditation is seen by the world of education as less rigorous than traditional regional accreditation. Where a regionally accredited degree is explicitly required, as it often is for teaching licenses and graduate school applications, a DETC-accredited degree will not qualify. There are only a few DETC-accredited schools in this book, and they are marked as such.

DISTANCE EDUCATION AND TRAINING COUNCIL (DETC)

1601 18th Street NW
Washington, DC 20009
(202) 234 5100 • Fax: (202) 332 1386 • Web site: www.detc.org

Professional accreditation

Unlike regional accreditors or the DETC, professional accrediting agencies represent a particular field of study, and therefore deal not with an entire college or university but with a particular department within that college or university. For example, the American Psychology Association accredits programs offered by psychology departments.

The National Council for Accreditation of Teacher Education (NCATE) is the relevant professional accreditor for the teaching field. With few exceptions, a teaching credential program must be NCATE-accredited to meet state licensing requirements. All of the credential programs listed in this book are approved by the NCATE.

NATIONAL COUNCIL FOR ACCREDITATION OF TEACHER EDUCATION (NCATE)

2010 Massachusetts Ave. NW
Washington, DC 20036
(202) 466 7496 • Web site: www.ncate.org

One specialized area of education where professional accreditation carries some importance is librarianship. Where applicable, we've noted in the listings which programs are accredited by the American Library Association:

AMERICAN LIBRARY ASSOCIATION

50 East Huron St.
Chicago, IL 60611
(312) 280 2432 • Web site: www.ala.org

"Down by the Oldstream Mill!
Where we sell degrees,
No forms finer than these,
Just as neat as you please!
Ed.D. in a breeze,
Your pay scale will increase!
So we'll send you our bill,
From here, all is uphill,
Down by the Oldstream Mill!"

"International accreditation"

As we discuss earlier, accreditation is an American phenomenon and has no meaning outside the U.S. There is no such thing as an "international accreditor," and any organization that claims to be one is probably bogus.

So how is legitimacy determined for non-U.S. schools? In general, if a school is approved or operated by the government of the country in which it is based, it is recognized as equivalent to a regionally accredited school in the U.S. There are exceptions to this: Some countries—certain Caribbean island nations come to mind—have been known to approve schools whose quality is more than suspect. For more specific information on how to determine the legitimacy of a foreign school, see this chapter's sidebar, "How to check out a school not in this book."

Of course, all of the foreign schools listed in this book are internationally respected and accepted. For the accreditation field of their individual listings, we've given them the designation "Non-U.S. equivalent."

For Personal Advice on Your Own Situation

If you would like advice and recommendations on your own specific situation, a personal counseling service offers this information, by mail only. John started this service in 1977 at the request of many readers. While he still remains a consultant, since 1981 the actual consulting and personal evaluations have been done by two colleagues of his, who are leading experts in the field of nontraditional education.

For a modest consulting fee, these things are done:

▶ You will get a long personal letter evaluating your situation, recommending the best degree programs for you (including part-time programs in your area, if relevant), and estimating how long it will take and what it will cost you to complete your degree(s).

▶ You will get answers to any specific questions you may have with regard to programs you may now be considering, institutions you have already dealt with, or other relevant matters.

▶ You will get detailed, up-to-the-minute information on institutions and degree programs, equivalency exams, sources of the correspondence courses you may need, career opportunities, resumé writing, sources of financial aid, and other topics in the form of extensive prepared notes.

▶ You will be entitled to telephone the service for a full year for unlimited follow-up counseling, to keep updated on new programs and other changes, and to otherwise use the service as your personal information resource.

If you are interested in this personal counseling, please write or call and you will be sent descriptive literature and a counseling questionnaire, without cost or obligation.

If, once you have these materials, you do want counseling, simply fill out the questionnaire and return it, with a letter and resumé if you like, along with the fee. Your personal reply and counseling materials will be airmailed to you as quickly as possible.

For free information about this service, write, telephone, or email:

Degree Consulting Services
P.O. Box 3533
Santa Rosa, CA 95402

Phone: (707) 539 6466
Fax: (707) 538 3577
Email: degrees@sonic.net
Web site: www.degreeconsult.com

APPENDIX E

Bending the Rules

One of the most common complaints or admonishments we hear from readers goes something like this: "You said thus-and-so, but when I inquired of the school, they told me such-and-such." It has happened (although rarely) that a school claims that a program we have written about does not exist. Sometimes a student achieves something (such as completing a certain degree entirely by correspondence) that we have been told by a high official of the school was impossible.

One of the open secrets in the world of higher education is that the rules are constantly being bent. But as with the Emperor's new clothes, no one dares to point and say what is really going on, especially in print.

Unfortunately, we cannot provide many specific examples of bent rules, naming names and all. This is for two good reasons:

1. Many situations where students profit from bent rules would disappear in an instant if anyone dared mention the situation publicly. There is, for instance, a major state university that is forbidden by its charter from granting degrees for correspondence study. But they regularly work out special arrangements for students who are carried on the books as residential students even though all work is done by mail. Indeed, some graduates have never set foot on campus. If this ever got out, the Board of Trustees, the relevant accrediting agency, and all the other universities in that state would probably have conniptions, and the practice would be suspended at once.

2. These kinds of things can change so rapidly, particularly with new personnel or new policies, that a listing of anomalies and curious practices would probably be obsolete before the ink dried.

Consider a few examples of the sort of thing that is going on in higher education every day, whether or not anyone will admit it (except perhaps behind closed doors or after a few drinks):

▶ A friend of John's at a major university was unable to complete one required course for her doctorate before she had to leave for another state. This university does not offer correspondence courses, but she was able to convince a professor to enroll her in a regular course, which she would just happen never to visit in person.

▶ A man in graduate school needed to be enrolled in nine units of coursework each semester to keep his employer's tuition-assistance plan going. But his job was too demanding one year, and he was unable to do so. The school enrolled him in nine units of "independent study" for which no work was asked or required, and for which a "pass" grade was given.

- A woman at a large school needed to get a certain number of units before an inflexible time deadline. When it was clear she was not going to make it, a kindly professor turned in grades for her, and told her she could do the actual coursework later on.

- A major state university offers nonresident degrees for people living in that state only. When a reader wrote to John saying that he, living a thousand miles from that state, was able to complete his degree entirely by correspondence, we asked a contact at that school exactly what was going on. "We will take students from anywhere in our correspondence degree program," she told us. "But for God's sake, don't print that in your book, or we'll be deluged with applicants."

Please use this information prudently. It will probably do no good to pound on a table and say, "What do you mean, I can't do this? John Bear says that rules don't mean anything anyway." But when faced with a problem, it can surely do no harm to remember that there do exist many situations in which the rules have turned out to be far less rigid than the printed literature of a school would lead you to believe.

Cheerleading tryouts at a
University Without Walls program.

Bibliography

Most of these books are available in bookstores and libraries, on the Internet through services like *www.amazon.com*, and from a large service that specializes in providing books to distance education students: Specialty Books, 5833 Industrial Drive, Athens, OH 45701; phone: (800) 466 1365 or (740) 594 2274; fax: (740) 593 3045; *www.specialty-books.com*. Some, however, are sold only or primarily by mail. In those cases we have given ordering information. In addition, some highly recommended books are now out of print. If you feel from the description that they would be useful in your situation, try your local library, a good second-hand bookstore, or some of the Web sites that deal in used books such as *www.bookfinder.com* or *www.abebooks.com*. Where we have prices and other information, we've given it, though of course these things are always subject to change.

General Reference Books

The ones we use every day

Bears' Guide to Earning Degrees by Distance Learning (Ten Speed Press, (800) 841 2665). What, you thought we didn't use our own book? In print for over 25 years, this is the "mother" publication of the *Bears' Guide* series and profiles over 2,500 schools that offer nontraditional programs in virtually all fields, from accounting to Zulu. We also go into more depth on issues such as alternative means of earning credit, accreditation and state licensure, honorary doctorates, non-U.S. schools, and research doctorates. 432 pages, $30.

Higher Education Directory (Higher Education Publications, 6400 Arlington Blvd., Suite 648, Falls Church, VA 22042; (703) 532 2300; *www.hepinc.com*). A massive yearly publication that gives detailed factual information (no opinions or ratings) on all accredited schools. More than 800 pages, $64.

International Handbook of Universities (Groves Dictionaries). Gives detailed information on virtually every college, university, technical institute, and training school in the world. This is the book that is most used by collegiate registrars and admissions officers to evaluate schools. 1,500 pages, $250.

Commonwealth Universities Yearbook (Association of Commonwealth Universities, London; distributed in the U.S. by Stockton Press, New York). This standard reference work covers what it refers to as all schools "in good standing" in 36 countries or areas. Many admissions departments use this book in making admissions or acceptance decisions. More than 600 institutions are described in great detail. More than 2,500 pages, $265.

The others

Accredited Institutions of Postsecondary Education (Oryx Press). Issued around the middle of each year, this book lists every accredited institution and candidate for accreditation. This is the book many people use to determine conclusively whether or not a given American school is accredited. 735 pages, $70.

Barron's Profiles of American Colleges (Barron's Educational Series). A massive 1,300-page volume that describes every accredited college and university in America, with lists of majors offered by each school.

Campus-Free College Degrees by Marcie K. Thorson (Thorson Guides). This well-done book covers much of the same territory as *Bears' Guide*, but accredited U.S.-based schools only, with considerably longer descriptions of each.

College Degrees by Mail and Internet by John and Mariah Bear (Ten Speed Press). Our publisher asked for a smaller and less comprehensive book on the topic, and this is it. We select 100 accredited schools with the best distance-degree programs, and write them up in more detail. 205 pages, $15.

A Guide to College Programs in Teacher Preparation (NCATE, 1999). This book lists all of the National Council for Accreditation of Teacher Education (NCATE) programs in the U.S. Almost without exception, a school must have NCATE accreditation in order to have a teacher education program. The book includes contact information and the degrees/programs offered by each school. Unfortunately, due to the dearth of credential programs available via distance, they don't currently have a "distance learning" category. We hope that subsequent issues will.

The Independent Study Catalog (Peterson's Guides). A master catalog listing 13,000 correspondence courses offered by more than 140 U.S. and Canadian institutions. Was updated regularly through 1998 but is now out of print.

Peterson's Guide to Distance Learning Programs (Peterson's Guides). Probably the main competitor to *Bears' Guide*, this is quite a comprehensive collection of information. Covers associate's and nondegree programs (which we don't); does not cover unaccredited schools or schools outside North America (which we do). Our real annoyance with this book is that more than one quarter of it, 200 pages, is taken up with paid advertising for schools, which until 2000 (when the practice finally came under some scrutiny from the press) was never identified as paid advertising, but simply as "in-depth descriptions." "It never occurred to us this is something we should highlight," explained Cristopher Maloney, Peterson's senior vice president for marketing.

Peterson's Guide to Four-Year Colleges (Peterson's Guides). Another massive annual directory covering traditional accredited schools only.

Peterson's Guide to Graduate and Professional Programs (Peterson's Guides). Five large books, each describing in detail opportunities for residential graduate study in the U.S. Volumes cover social science and humanities, biological and agricultural sciences, physical sciences, and engineering. There is also a summary volume. The series is updated annually.

World-Wide Inventory of Non-Traditional Degree Programs (UNESCO, c/o Unipub, 4611-F Assembly Dr., Lanham, MD 20706-4391; (800) 274 4447; *www.bernan.com*).

A generally useful United Nations report on what many of the world's nations are doing in the way of nontraditional education. Some helpful school descriptions, and lots of detailed descriptions of evening courses offered by workers' cooperatives in Bulgaria and suchlike.

World Guide to Higher Education (Bowker Publishing Co.). A comprehensive survey by the United Nations of educational systems, degrees, and qualifications, from Afghanistan to Zambia.

Credit for Life Experience

Earn College Credit for What You Know by Lois Lamdin (Kendall/Hunt Publishing Company). How to put together a life-experience portfolio: how to gather the necessary information, document it, and assemble it. $25.

National Guide to Educational Credit for Training Programs (Oryx Press). Many non-traditional programs use this large volume, based on American Council on Education recommendations, to assign credit for more than 5,000 business, trade union, association, and government agency training programs. 1,200 pages, $85.

Guide to the Evaluation of Educational Experiences in the Armed Forces (Oryx Press). Many schools use this 2,000-page 3-volume set (one for each service) to assess credit for nonschool learning. Describes and makes credit recommendations for more than 8,000 military training programs.

Portfolio Development and Adult Learning: Purposes and Strategies by Alan Mandell and Elana Michelson (Council for Adult and Experiential Learning). Explores the eight approaches to portfolio development courses most typically used at colleges and universities, providing examples of each through a closer examination of prior learning assessment programs offered at 11 institutions of higher learning.

Prior Learning Assessment: The Portfolio by Marthe Sansregret (Hurtubise HMH, LaSalle, Quebec). A well-respected head of assessment for a major university told us that this is the book he asks his students to use to create their portfolios. It comes with software (Mac or DOS) to make the process more efficient. No longer in print, and the publisher appears to have gone out of business, so it may take some sleuthing to find a copy.

Financial Aid

The A's and B's of Academic Scholarships by Anna Leider (Octameron Associates). Lists more than 100,000 scholarships plus advice on earning them.

Don't Miss Out: The Ambitious Student's Guide to Financial Aid by Anna and Robert Leider (Octameron Associates). This one gives excellent advice (in 144 pages for $10) in pursuing the traditional route to financial aid.

Finding Money for College by John Bear and Mariah Bear (Ten Speed Press). We collected all the information we could find about the nontraditional and unorthodox approaches to getting a share in the billions of dollars that go unclaimed each year, including barter, real estate and tax gambits, negotiation, creative payment plans, obscure scholarships, foundations that make grants to individuals, etc. Any bookseller can supply or order this book.

The Scholarship Book by Daniel Cassidy (Prentice-Hall), *Dan Cassidy's Worldwide College Scholarship Directory,* and *Dan Cassidy's Worldwide Graduate Scholarship Directory* (Career Press). These three books are, in effect, a complete printout of the data banks of information used by Cassidy's National Scholarship Research Service. Tens of thousands of sources are listed for undergraduate and graduate students, for study in the U.S. and overseas.

Miscellany

The External Degree as a Credential: Graduates' Experiences in Employment and Further Study by Carol Sosdian and Laure Sharp (National Institute of Education). This 1978 report is probably the most often misquoted and misinterpreted educational survey ever published. Many schools (some good, some not) cite the findings (a high satisfaction level for external students and a high acceptance level for external degrees) without mentioning it related only to fully accredited undergraduate degrees, and has little or no relevance to unaccredited undergraduate or graduate degrees.

Get Your Degree Online by Matthew and April Helm (McGraw-Hill, 2000). A readable, user-friendly book that focuses mainly on undergraduate and certificate programs. $22.

Getting What You Came For: The Smart Student's Guide to Earning a Master's or Ph.D. by Robert L. Peters, Ph.D. (Noonday Press, 1997). Another wonderful and extremely helpful book. Quoting from the first chapter, "Graduate students run into problems because they do not understand how graduate school works, nor do most undergraduate counselors and graduate departments provide enough realistic guidance. . . . This book tells you what graduate school is really like. . . . I tell you how to create a comprehensive strategy that blends politics, psychology, and planning to ensure that your hard work pays off with a degree and a job." And he does, eloquently.

The Ph.D. Trap Revisited by Wilfred Cude (Dundurn Press). The author was treated very badly in his own graduate program, which turned him into a reformer. Farley Mowat writes that he is "the kind of reformer this world needs. Humane, literate, reasonable, and utterly implacable, he has just unmasked the gruesome goings on in the academic morgue that deals in doctoral degrees. Any student contemplating the pursuit of a doctorate had better read *The Ph.D. Trap* as a matter of basic self-preservation. . . ."

"Well, no, I've never unrolled it; I'm allergic to Asterolasia hexapetala. *But gosh, isn't that a pretty ribbon?"*

Virtual College by Pam Dixon (Peterson's, 1996). A charming and very helpful little book (and she says nice things about *Bears' Guide*, too), focusing on many of the issues the distance learner may face, including transfer of credits, employer acceptance, listing distance degrees on a resumé, choosing technology, what it is like to be a distance student, and so on. $10.

Internet Resources

It is not surprising that what is fast becoming the primary medium *of* distance learning is exploding into the primary resource for information *about* distance learning. Internet sites, however, come and go with the morning dew, so we've decided that the best place for keeping up with what's on the Net is on the Net itself. Start your search for online resources at the Bears' Guide Web site—*www.degree.net*—where we'll keep fresh and up-to-date our list of the best discussion groups, school directories, listservs, and Web-posted news items in the world of distance learning.

That said, another excellent starting point is the About.com Distance Learning Forum (*distancelearn.about.com*), which provides a wealth of useful information and links; and *www.degreeinfo.com*, a very popular moderated distance-learning forum to which a few of this book's authors frequently contribute.

SUBJECT INDEX

B=Bachelor's • M=Master's • D=Doctorate • C=Certificate • S=Specialist • NR=Nonresident • SR=Short Residency

University of Illinois at Urbana-Champaign (M, NR, 50)
University of Nebraska—Lincoln (D, SR, 96)
University of New England (D, NR, 100)
University of Phoenix (M, NR, 50)
University of Sarasota (S, SR, 79)

Deaf Education
University of Manchester (M, NR, 72; C, SR, 87)

Distance Education
Athabasca University (M, NR, 51; C, NR, 82)
California State University—Hayward (M, NR, 51; C, NR, 83)
Capella University (M, NR, 52; C, NR, 83; D, SR, 93)
Curtin University of Technology (M, NR, 52)
Florida State University (M, NR, 64)
Jones International University (M, NR, 52; C, NR, 83)
Marlboro College (M, SR, 52; C, SR, 83)
Nova Southeastern University (M, SR, 53; D, SR, 94)
Open University (M, NR, 53)
Royal Roads University (M, SR, 53)
University of London (M, NR, 53)
University of Maryland (M, NR, 54; C, NR, 83)
University of Phoenix (M, NR, 54)
University of Southern Queensland (M, NR, 54; C, NR, 84)

Early Childhood Education
Atlantic Union College (B, SR, 11)
Central Queensland University (B, NR, 13)
Charles Sturt University (B, NR, 13)
Concordia University (M, SR, 58; C, NR, 88)
Edith Cowan University (M, NR, 58)
Macquarie University (B, NR, 15; D, NR, 97)

Nova Southeastern University (B, SR, 19; M, SR, 59)
St. Mary-of-the-Woods College (B, SR, 20)
University of South Africa (B, NR, 17; M, NR, 59)
University of South Australia (B, NR, 18; C, NR, 89; D, NR, 100)
University of Wyoming (C, NR, 89)

Early Childhood Special Education
Emporia State University (C, NR, 88)

Education (General)
Australian Catholic University (D, NR, 96)
Capella University (M, NR, 39; D, SR, 93)
Central Queensland University (M, NR, 39)
Charles Sturt University (M, NR, 39)
College of St. Scholastica (M, SR, 39)
Curtin University of Technology (B, NR, 13)
Deakin University (M, NR, 40)
Edith Cowan University (M, NR, 40; D, NR, 97)
Flinders University (D, NR, 97)
Liberty University (M, SR, 40)
Monash University (M, NR, 41)
Northern Territory University (B, NR, 15)
Nova Southeastern University (B, SR, 19)
Open University (B, NR, 16; M, NR, 41; D, NR, 97)
Open University of Hong Kong (D, NR, 94)
Prescott College (B, SR, 20; M, SR, 41)
Regent University (M, NR, 41)
South Bank University (M, SR, 42; D, SR, 98)
Stephens College (B, SR, 16)
Universidad Estatal a Distancia (B, NR, 16)
Universidad Nacional de Educacion a Distancia (D, SR, 95)
University of Bradford (M, SR, 42; D, SR, 98)
University of Manchester (D, SR, 98)

University of Melbourne (M, SR, 42; D, SR, 100)
University of New England (D, NR, 100)
University of Pretoria (B, NR, 17; M, SR, 42)
University of Sarasota (M, SR, 43)
University of South Africa (B, NR, 17; M, NR, 43; D, NR, 100)
University of South Australia (D, NR, 100)
University of Southern Queensland (B, NR, 18; M, NR, 43)
University of Tasmania (M, SR, 43; D, SR, 102)
University of Wales—Aberystwyth (M, SR, 43; D, SR, 102)
Walden University (D, SR, 96)

Education Law and Policy
Franklin Pierce Law Center (M, SR, 75; C, SR, 88)
University of Illinois at Urbana-Champaign (M, NR, 76)

Educational Psychology
Texas A&M University—Commerce (D, SR, 95)
University of South Africa (M, NR, 76; D, NR, 100)

Educational Technology
Boise State University (M, NR, 54)
City University (M, NR, 54)
Edith Cowan University (M, NR, 55)
Emporia State University (M, NR, 55)
Florida Gulf Coast University (M, NR, 55)
George Washington University (M, NR, 55)
Jones International University (M, NR, 52; C, NR, 83)
Lesley University (M, NR, 68)
Marlboro College (M, SR, 52; C, SR, 83)
Nova Southeastern University (M, SR, 55; D, SR, 94)
Pepperdine University (M, SR, 56; D, SR, 94)
University of Illinois at Urbana-Champaign (M, NR, 56)

B=Bachelor's • M=Master's • D=Doctorate • C=Certificate • S=Specialist • NR=Nonresident • SR=Short Residency

Educational Technology (cont.)
University of Manchester (M, NR, 56)

University of Maryland (M, NR, 56; C, NR, 83)

University of Melbourne (M, SR, 57)

University of Northern Iowa (M, SR, 57)

University of Phoenix (M, NR, 57)

University of Pretoria (M, SR, 57)

University of South Alabama (M, NR, 57)

University of Southern Queensland (M, NR, 57; C, NR, 84)

University of Tennessee—Chattanooga (S, SR, 79)

University of Texas (M, NR, 58)

University of Wyoming (M, NR, 58)

Valdosta State University (S, NR, 80)

Walden University (M, SR, 58)

Elementary Education
Charles Sturt University (B, NR, 13)

Deakin University (B, NR, 13)

Judson College (B, NR, 19)

Liberty University (M, SR, 59)

Nova Southeastern University (B, SR, 19)

Open University of Hong Kong (B, NR, 16)

St. Mary-of-the-Woods College (B, SR, 20)

University of Northern Iowa (B, SR, 17)

University of South Africa (B, NR, 17; M, NR, 59)

Environmental Education
Deakin University (M, NR, 67)

Edith Cowan University (M, NR, 68)

Prescott College (M, SR, 69)

University of Saskatchewan (C, NR, 87)

English as a Second Language (ESL)
See Teaching English

Gerontology Education
Lakehead University (M, NR, 75)

Gifted Education
Nova Southeastern University (B, SR, 19)

University of South Africa (B, NR, 17; M, NR, 73)

University of South Alabama (M, NR, 73; C, NR, 88)

Guidance Counseling and School Psychology
Capella University (M, SR, 73; C, SR, 88; D, SR, 93)

Liberty University (M, SR, 75)

University of South Africa (B, NR, 17; M, NR, 76)

University of Southern Queensland (D, NR, 100)

Health Education
College of West Virginia (B, NR, 22)

Deakin University (M, NR, 67)

Nova Southeastern University (D, SR, 94)

Thomas Edison State College (B, NR, 16)

University of Dundee (M, NR, 69; C, NR, 86)

University of Illinois at Chicago (M, SR, 69)

University of Melbourne (M, SR, 70; D, SR, 100)

University of South Africa (M, NR, 70)

History of Education
University of South Africa (M, NR, 76; D, NR, 100)

Information Technology Education
Deakin University (M, NR, 67)

University of Melbourne (M, SR, 70; D, SR, 100)

Instruction
See Teaching

Instructional Technology
See Educational Technology

International Education
Monash University (M, NR, 75)

University of South Africa (M, NR, 76)

Language and Literacy Education
Deakin University (M, NR, 61)

Griffith University (B, NR, 15)

Edith Cowan University (M, NR, 61)

Open University (D, NR, 97)

University of Melbourne (M, SR, 62; D, SR, 100)

See also Reading and Literacy Education

See also Teaching English

See also Teaching Languages Other Than English

Leadership
See Administration

Library and Information Science
Charles Sturt University (M, NR, 63)

Connecticut State University (M, NR, 63)

Curtin University of Technology (M, NR, 63)

Drexel University (M, NR, 64)

Emporia State University (M, SR, 64)

Florida State University (M, NR, 64)

Jones International University (M, NR, 52)

Syracuse University (M, SR, 64)

University of Arizona (M, SR, 65)

University of Nothern Iowa (M, SR, 65)

University of Wisconsin—Milwaukee (M, NR, 65)

Mathematics Education
Deakin University (M, NR, 67)

Edith Cowan University (M, NR, 68)

Montana State University—Bozeman (M, SR, 69)

University of Idaho (M, NR, 69)

University of Melbourne (M, SR, 70; D, SR, 100)

University of Northern Iowa (M, SR, 70)

University of South Africa (M, NR, 70)

Middle School Education
University of Northern Iowa (M, SR, 59)

B=Bachelor's • M=Master's • D=Doctorate • C=Certificate • S=Specialist • NR=Nonresident • SR=Short Residency

Music Education

Duquesne University (M, SR, 68)

Edith Cowan University (M, NR, 68)

Judson College (B, NR, 19)

University of Pretoria (M, SR, 70)

Philosophy of Education

University of South Africa (M, NR, 76; D, NR, 100)

Physical Education

Atlantic Union College (B, SR, 11)

Deakin University (M, NR, 67)

Eastern Oregon University (B, NR, 14)

Emporia State University (M, NR, 68)

University of Melbourne (M, SR, 70; D, SR, 100)

Virginia Polytechnic Institute and State University (M, NR, 70)

Reading and Literacy Education

City University (M, NR, 60)

Deakin University (M, NR, 61)

Edith Cowan University (M, NR, 61)

Liberty University (M, SR, 61)

University of Northern Iowa (M, SR, 63)

University of Texas (M, NR, 63)

See also **Language and Literacy Education**

Religious Education

Concordia University (M, SR, 65) [Christian]

Edith Cowan University (M, NR, 66) [Interfaith/Christian]

Global University of the Assemblies of God (B, NR, 14; M, NR, 66; C, NR, 86) [Christian]

Griggs University (B, NR, 15; C, NR, 86) [Christian]

Judson College (B, NR, 19) [Christian]

Maryvale Institute (B, SR, 15; M, SR, 66; D, SR, 97) [Christian: Roman Catholic]

Naropa University (M, SR, 66) [Interfaith/Buddhist]

Oral Roberts University (B, NR, 19) [Christian]

Regent University (M, NR, 67) [Christian]

Spertus College (M, NR, 67) [Jewish]

University of Glasgow (M, NR, 67; C, NR, 87) [Interfaith/Christian]

School Psychology

See **Guidance Counseling and School Psychology**

School Security

Regent University (M, SR, 76)

Science Education

Curtin University of Technology (M, NR, 67)

Deakin University (M, NR, 67)

Edith Cowan University (M, NR, 68)

Lesley University (M, NR, 68)

Montana State University— Bozeman (M, SR, 69)

Nova Southeastern University (B, SR, 19)

University of South Africa (M, NR, 70)

Secondary Education

Deakin University (B, NR, 13)

Judson College (B, NR, 19)

Liberty University (M, SR, 59)

Nova Southeastern University (B, SR, 19)

Open University of Hong Kong (B, NR, 16)

St. Mary-of-the-Woods College (B, SR, 20)

University of South Africa (M, NR, 59)

Social Studies Education

Deakin University (M, NR, 67)

Edith Cowan University (M, NR, 68)

Sociology of Education

University of South Africa (M, NR, 76; D, NR, 100)

Spanish for Teachers

California State University— Hayward (C, NR, 84)

Special Education

Charles Sturt University (M, NR, 71)

Deakin University (M, NR, 71)

Edith Cowan University (M, NR, 71)

Emporia State University (C, NR, 87)

Flinders University (B, NR, 14; M, NR, 71)

Liberty University (M, SR, 72)

Nova Southeastern University (B, SR, 19)

Open University (M, NR, 72; C, NR, 87; D, NR, 97)

St. Mary-of-the-Woods College (B, SR, 20)

University of Birmingham (B, NR, 17; C, NR, 87; D, SR, 98)

University of New England (D, NR, 100)

University of Northern Iowa (M, SR, 72)

University of South Africa (D, NR, 100)

University of Southern Queensland (D, NR, 100)

Teaching

Capella University (M, NR, 49; D, SR, 93)

City University (M, NR, 49)

Edith Cowan University (M, NR, 49)

Fielding Institute (D, SR, 93)

Florida Gulf Coast University (M, NR, 55)

Grand Canyon University (M, NR, 49)

Liberty University (D, SR, 93)

Open University (D, NR, 97)

Prescott College (B, SR, 20)

St. Joseph's College (M, SR, 41)

University of Maryland (M, NR, 50)

University of Nebraska—Lincoln (D, SR, 96)

University of Sarasota (S, SR, 79)

University of Technology, Sydney (D, NR, 102)

Walden University (M, SR, 51)

Teaching English

Aston University (M, NR, 60; C, NR, 84)

Azusa Pacific University (M, SR, 60)

California State University— Fresno (C, NR, 84)

Deakin University (M, NR, 61)

B=Bachelor's • M=Master's • D=Doctorate • C=Certificate • S=Specialist • NR=Nonresident • SR=Short Residency

Teaching English (cont.)
Emporia State University (C, NR, 85)
Florida Gulf Coast University (C, NR, 85)
New School University (C, NR, 85)
Open University (D, NR, 97)
Regent University (M, SR, 62; C, NR, 85)
University of Leicester (M, NR, 62; C, NR, 85)
University of Manchester (M, NR, 62; C, NR, 86)
University of Melbourne (M, SR, 62; D, SR, 100)
University of Saskatchewan (C, NR, 86)
University of Texas (C, NR, 86)

Teaching English to Students of Other Languages (TESOL)
See **Teaching English**

Teaching Languages Other Than English
Deakin University (M, NR, 61)

Technology Education
Edith Cowan University (M, NR, 68)
Lesley University (M, NR, 68)
Nova Southeastern University (D, SR, 94)
See also **Information Technology Education**

Vocational Education
Capella University (M, NR, 47; C, NR, 81)
Central Queensland University (B, NR, 13)
Charles Sturt University (B, NR, 13)
Edith Cowan University (M, NR, 47)
Griffith University (B, NR, 15; C, NR, 81)
Jones International University (M, NR, 52)
Nova Southeastern University (D, SR, 94)
Open University (D, NR, 97)

University of Central Florida (B, NR, 17)
University of Southern Queensland (B, NR, 18; C, NR, 82)
University of Technology, Sydney (D, NR, 102)
Virginia Polytechnic Institute and State University (C, NR, 82)
See also **Adult Education**

Women's Studies Education
Lakehead University (M, NR, 75)
Open University (D, NR, 97)

Youth Studies and Youth Work
Brunel University (B, NR, 12; M, NR, 73)
Concordia University (B, SR, 13; M, SR, 73)
Edith Cowan University (B, NR, 14)
Nova Southeastern University (M, SR, 75; D, SR, 94)
University of Victoria (B, NR, 18)
See also **Child Development and Child Care**

B=Bachelor's • M=Master's • D=Doctorate • C=Certificate • S=Specialist • NR=Nonresident • SR=Short Residency

GENERAL INDEX